Flying the Hump

The War Diary of Peter H. Dominick

Edited by Alexander S. Dominick

M&B Global Solutions, Inc.
Green Bay, Wisconsin (USA)

Flying the Hump
The War Diary of Peter H. Dominick

© 2018 Alexander S. Dominick

First Edition
All Rights Reserved. The author grants no assignable permission to reproduce for resale or redistribution. This license is limited to the individual purchaser and does not extend to others. Permission to reproduce these materials for any other purpose must be obtained in writing from the publisher except for the use of brief quotations within book chapters.

Disclaimer
The views expressed in this work are solely those of the author and the deceased author of the diary and short story reproduced within. They do not necessarily reflect the views of the publisher, and the publisher hereby disclaims any responsibility for them. In the event you use any of the information in this book for yourself, which is your constitutional right, the author and the publisher assume no responsibility for your actions.

Front cover photo of Peter H. Dominick and Nancy Parks Dominick with their two eldest children, Peter Hoyt Dominick Jr. and Michael Parks Dominick, from the family collection.

Back cover photo courtesy USAF, via Air Mobility Command Museum, Dover Air Force Base, Delaware.

All photos are from the Dominick family collection unless otherwise noted.

ISBN-13: 978-1-942731-32-0
ISBN-10: 1-942731-32-9

Published by M&B Global Solutions Inc.
Green Bay, Wisconsin (USA)

Dedication

To my dear mother, who left this world on February 2, 2015.

I wish you were here to read this. We miss you. Your love, laughter, and support made us all better.

This was my mother's engagement picture. She was twenty years old. Dad carried it with him everywhere.

Contents

Introduction 1
Diary - Part 1 9
Diary - Part 2 27
Diary - Part 3 47
Diary - Part 4 69
Diary - Part 5 83
Diary - Part 6 95
"The Rock Pile" - A short story 103
Afterword 127
Acknowledgements 135

Introduction

My father, Peter H. Dominick, was born on July 7, 1915. Over the course of his sixty-five years, he was by turn a rebellious youth, above-average student, attorney, pilot, veteran of World War II, community leader, U.S. Congressman, U.S. Senator, and briefly the U.S. Ambassador to Switzerland before being sidelined by multiple sclerosis and eventually succumbing to the disease.

This is my favorite picture of my father, Peter H. Dominick, taken about 1965 while he was a U.S. Senator for the state of Colorado.

Details of his public career are readily available, but the military service that shaped his subsequent life of public service was largely unknown, even within our family.

He was a very passionate man who held strong opinions about a variety of topics. He determined early on that he wanted to move west and decline the expected career trajectory of joining the family's investment banking firm Dominick & Dominick in New York. After the war, he and Mom visited several cities and ultimately decided to settle in Denver, Colorado. They were captivated by the wide-open spaces, endless vistas, and numerous opportunities to explore the Rocky Mountains by hiking, camping, skiing, fishing, and hunting.

During the course of sorting through his belongings following his death in 1981, my sister, Lynne, discovered a small brown notebook about five inches long and three inches wide. It was his war diary, written in pencil, and no one had ever known of its existence until that moment. The first entry was dated midway through his deployment, meaning there likely was another volume yet undiscovered.

We began an exhaustive search to find the first part of this treasure, but after days of hunting through masses of boxes, drawers, closets, and cupboards, we finally gave up and settled for what we had. Lynne had a friend transcribe the penciled notes into a digital document and gave it to me to read.

My dad had been stationed in India with the US Army Air Corps, and his assignment was to fly supplies over the Himalayas into China to help the Chinese soldiers combat the advancing Japanese forces. The common name for these missions was "Flying the Hump." Another nickname was "The Aluminum Trail," because of the number of aircraft that crashed there.

The partial diary was a detailed daily accounting of his wartime experiences. It was by turns hair-raising and hilarious. We had heard many of his stories over the years, but not all of them. Not the ones that became evident in reading the diary. We knew his experience had been difficult and he had lost friends during the war. He had seen some amazing sights while he was stationed in India, but he had guarded against sharing the more terrifying moments he had endured. Like many men of his generation, he was a strong, silent type who did what had to be done no matter the difficulty, because it was the right thing to do.

It appeared he wished to keep the diaries private, as he never once mentioned their existence to anyone. My mother was as astounded as any of us when the first part was discovered. I edited and published the partial diary for private distribution among family members and friends in 1984. At the time, my motivation was to preserve his history and provide our family members with something interesting to read about a previously undisclosed period of Dad's life. It gave me something to do, since I was unemployed and thinking about becoming a writer.

When our family home was sold in August 2014, the first part of his diary miraculously appeared as we meticulously sorted through all the items in storage. This notebook was also written in pencil. In addition, we discovered a short story he had written called *The Rock Pile*, which is another name for the Himalayas. You will see this story at the end of his diary. We also uncovered a box of letters he had written home to Mom during his time in India.

I decided to transcribe, as best I could, the first half of his diary, combine the two volumes, and republish the complete journal of Dad's war-time experiences. Something very interesting happened as I worked through this task. I developed a new relationship with my father – one that transcended his death. I've described how that happened, and added details about my life and relationship with my father.

His diary and letters allowed me to follow his growth from a young man who had admittedly lived a privileged life, to a man who braved incredible hardships and terrifying moments on a daily basis, and whose patriotism and pride in American democracy and world leadership was hardened by his war-time experiences. His diary entries at first reflected what seem to be, at times, petty complaints about his lot and the poverty that surrounded him from the moment he left US soil and began his voyage to India.

These kinds of remarks grow less prevalent as he begins to experience the excruciatingly painful daily losses of friends and fellow pilots.

I had initially assumed that the small number of references to politics in his diary indicated he had yet to develop the fire in his belly for public service, but in the course of reviewing the letters he sent home to Mom during his time in India, I discovered that many of the principles he lived by and fought so hard for during his nineteen years of public service were already very evident.

Here is an excerpt from a letter he wrote home less than a month after he arrived at his post in India's Assam Valley:

"... I have thought for some time that the Army has done me a lot of good, making me less of an introvert and more of an extrovert, and interested in post-war problems less than in living a day-to-day existence. But, having very little to do most of the time over here, I've been thinking of all sorts of problems. I remarked the other day that I didn't feel like I had been worth any $360 a month to the government and that at times I was embarrassed to take it, pointing out that wages were supposedly paid for hard work, responsibility and ideas. In this game flying is mostly fun. There is quite a lot of work in it, but the off days are pretty numerous. The danger certainly doesn't compare to that of a private in the Marines attacking Tarawa. The responsibility consists of piloting a pretty valuable aeroplane with some four people in it and they pay you to train for that specific job as well as anyone can be trained ... (My bunkmate) believes that with only 600 hours to his credit, and most of that copilot time, that he has earned every cent and more and that everyone here should get the Congressional Medal of Honor for even being here. He thinks we're living a life of hardship, yet we have lanterns, a good roof, a satisfactory cot, all possible equipment, good (?) doctors, good planes, ample food, a native private servant and an occasional movie!

"Then there was the adolescent 2nd Lieutenant co-pilot of a B-17 in Memphis with (very little) education who remarked that 'We fighting men aren't going to stand for the government not taking care of us for the rest of our lives when this war is over!!'

It's an attitude that puzzles me, that thinks (sic) they are making an enormous sacrifice and are fighting for some race completely apart from themselves. They seem to have no conception that they're damn well in a privileged class to be able to fight, and that they are fighting for themselves and their own home which they used to love so much as well as for the 59th Street garment makers.

"I don't believe anyone, whether they are in the Army or in bars like Ike's joint or in the movies, wants this country to simply stand as it was.

"All sorts of things should be done. Probably some sort of taxation to more evenly distribute jobs earnings, some form of control over labor unions so that they don't act as racketeers and strike for plush seats on their work benches in the middle of a national emergency, some form of slum clearance and an adequate supervision of federal housing projects so that they don't turn into the slums which they were supposed to replace, an even more general educational system and an international peace force of some kind in which the U.S. and Great Britain are major partners. But all those things are merely plans which were formulated a long time ago by a lot of people. The war did nothing to bring them on except perhaps to make people see the necessity for them sooner rather they would have in times of peace and prosperity.

"I pray to Heaven that the young people have not lost their perception of the succession of advances or their sense of humor. If they think that after this the world owes them a living they're going to get an awful kick in the pants and I hope I'm there to help kick. The world owes no one unless he works for it. What I'm fighting for in a nutshell is to keep the Freedom of Speech that made me say such ridiculous things before the war was thrust upon us.

"Upon rereading I seem to have made a speech. I'm sorry darling."

Obviously, he was incapable of ignoring national issues and post-war problems, as he had hoped. But it is very clear he felt it imperative to speak out about what he felt needed to be done to maintain our American democracy.

The dangers involved with mountain flying are immense and constant. Air currents shift at alarming speed, weather changes in an instant, and the altitudes involved mean much thinner air and therefore increased difficulty achieving and maintaining proper altitudes. Flying the Hump has been described as the most treacherous route in aviation. It is worthwhile noting that thousands of American aircraft were lost during WWII in the China/Burma/India Theater, as well as nearly 1,000 pilots and other members of the flight crews.

The planes they flew were in a constant state of disrepair and much of the flying was done at night to avoid being detected and attacked by Japanese fighters. Since this concentrated effort was put in place only after the Burma Road was captured by the Japanese, effectively cutting off the land-based supply routes, these pilots often had to make it up as they went along. Route maps to the different Chinese airfields didn't exist, so if for some reason the navigational equipment malfunctioned, they had to navigate by instinct or what my father called "dead reckoning."

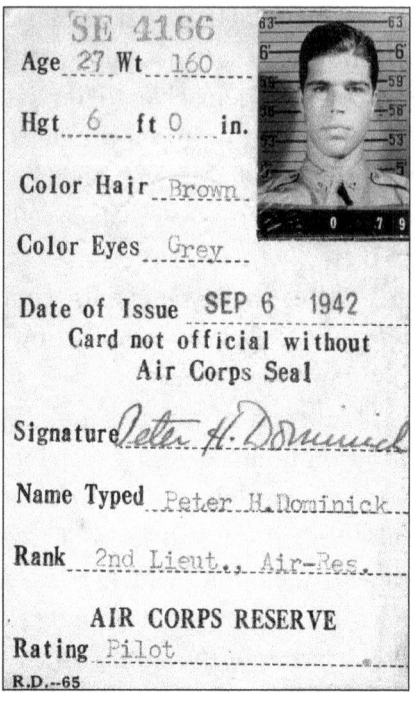

My dad's Air Corps Reserve ID card in the fall of 1942. (Image courtesy of Special Collections and Archives, University of Denver)

Add to that that the navigational equipment often malfunctioned due to thunderstorms, lightning strikes, icing, and any number of other meteorological or electrical issues, and you get a glimpse into the terrifying daily ordeals which he and his fellow crew members had to endure.

He had flown sixty-seven Hump missions by the time his service in India concluded. He also had used his legal training to defend several servicemen against various charges. He had made and lost lifelong friends. His hair, which had been jet black, turned salt and pepper (more salt than pepper.)

He requested a transfer to bomber duty – a request which thankfully was denied. Instead, he became a ferry pilot for the US Army Air Corps' Air Transport Command (ATC), moving planes from base to base as needed for the war effort.

Here then is the remarkable beginning of his story, unvarnished. It is my hope that you will appreciate learning how this statesman earned his wings.

Alexander S. Dominick

The Diary
Part 1

Cast of Frequent Characters

Marmie - His mother, Eleanor Hoyt Dominick
Boss - His father, Gayer G. Dominick
Nancy - His wife, Nancy Parks Dominick *(often as "Nance")*
Bud - His brother, Bayard Dominick
Betty - His brother's wife
Bud - His brother-in-law, Elton Parks

Inside the diary's cover were the following notations:
- National City Bank -
- Royal Dutch Shell -

Trip over, Memphis to Chabra, India
Ship 30590 C-87

Crew
Lt. Col. Estelli, Senior Pilot
Peter H. Dominick, Pilot
2nd Lt. Hi Randel, Co-Pilot
1st Lt. O.K. Brohaw, Navigator
M.Sgt. D.D. Wells, Crew Chief
Cpl. H.L. Aicholtz, Radio Operator

Alexander S. Dominick

ADDRESS REPLY TO
CHIEF OF THE AIR CORPS
WAR DEPARTMENT
WASHINGTON, D. C.

WAR DEPARTMENT
OFFICE OF THE CHIEF OF THE AIR CORPS   (1-B)
WASHINGTON

December 16, 1941

Mr. Peter H. Dominick
Carter, Ledyard & Milburn
2 Wall Street
New York, New York

Dear Sir:

        In reply to your letter of December 9, 1941, you are advised that under existing War Department regulations applicants to be eligible for appointment as Aviation Cadets in the Army Air Corps must be unmarried at the time of such appointment.

        However, in view of the fact that a change in this requirement is now under consideration, it is suggested that you send your application for this appointment direct to the Aviation Cadet Section, Office, Chief of Air Corps, attaching on the face thereof a copy of this letter. Your application should include three forms herewith enclosed, completed on both sides, three letters of recommendation, a certified copy of your birth certificate, and an official college transcript if you have attended college.

        As soon as official action has been taken on the appointment of married men as Aviation Cadets, your application will be forwarded to the appropriate Corps Area Headquarters for immediate action.

        Yours very truly,

        F. H. WALTON, JR.
        1st Lieut., Air Corps
        Asst. Chief, Aviation Cadet Section
        Military Personnel Division

Enc. 3

My father, Peter Dominick, received this response from the War Department regarding his request to enlist in the Army Air Corps two days after Pearl Harbor. (Image courtesy of Special Collections and Archives, University of Denver)

Memphis, Jan. 18, 1944
1) Secret Orders
2) Finance
3) Tire inspection record
4) Laundry
5) Get in touch with Bill Allen

Jan. 19 - Left Memphis in afternoon after kissing Marmie and Nancy and Boss goodbye. Arrived Maxwell Field for the second time since cadet days - still don't like it.

Jan. 20 - Left Maxwell for Miami. Col. and I are alternating days in flying ship. Met Betty in Miami and called Bud. He expects to leave for England tonight or tomorrow. Betty leaves tomorrow to try and see him before he goes. Went on spree with Betty to Little Palm Club.

Jan. 21 - Leisurely day on the beach with the Col., O.K. Brohaw and Hi Randel. Had a few drinks and went to bed for early flight tomorrow. Couldn't get Nance on the phone.

Jan. 22 - Left Miami and flew to Borenquin Field, Puerto Rico. No sign of two B-26s reported down en route. The Col. got 4 cases of liquor and Hi and I each got a case of rum and a couple of bottles of Canadian Club. Liquor cheap and plentiful here.

Jan. 23 - Left Borenquin and flew through dirty weather to Atkinson Field, Georgetown, British Guiana. Col. made me do an instrument let-down to field. Came out OK. Real jungle here - from here on all beds are equipped with mosquito nets. Must be a lonely post as town is 20 miles away.

Jan. 24 - Crossed equator today for first time. Country either thick jungle or desert beaches. Flew through tropical front which is perpetual near equator and all the way across the ocean. The

Col. sleeps while I try to fly instruments from right side. It's tough.

Went to town, Belem, Brazil - second biggest city in Brazil and still a dirty little native village. Got some silk stockings for Nance, by dint of gestures, and some French. Mostly sign language, which got embarrassing when dealing with sales girls.

Jan. 25 - Arrived Natal, Brazil, our takeoff point for ocean hop. Big post but dull. Country very deserty and the natives are dirty. Rotten food.

Jan. 26 - Plane being overhauled – they're trying to fix autopilot. Went to the beach and got sunburned to a crisp. Saw a bum movie.

It amazes me the amount of equipment the Army has at these posts.

Jan. 27 - Plane still not ready. Went to the beach again with the Col. and bought some table and glass mats at an exorbitant price after cutting the asking price in half.

Sat through a rain storm to see a movie. Couldn't get to town but Col. went and said it was dull.

Jan. 28 - Flew to Ascension – that's really a small frog in a big puddle. One tree on it and the rest volcanic rock. The British said a runway couldn't be built so American engineers put in a 6,000-foot runway in 3 months. It's up and down hill, but probably the most valuable spot in the system. The twin engines could never make the whole hop with any load. The story is that the French fleet started to attack at one point and then turned back. Subs have sat around here and shot planes down, but the patrol has scared most of them off. That's one hop a navigator is really useful on, though they do have a strong range on it. It's a spot about 4 miles long after an 1,800-mile flight.

Jan. 29 – Left early and flew through equatorial front again. Pretty rough weather – landed at Accra, British West Africa. They have a "harmattan," which is a dust condition cutting visibility to ¼ to 2 miles.

The natives here look just like South Carolina blacks. Our quarters are pretty good. The farther we go the more efficient things get. Got stabbed for typhus against an epidemic up the line in Aden.

Jan. 30 – Held over on account of the harmattan. Couldn't see a mile even on the ground. Went to town. Filled with blacks, mostly naked or equipped with G-strings or the women with a type of sarong. Naturally we drew guides like flies to molasses. It was Sunday, so everything was closed except the native market. They sell everything, but most of the stuff is imported from Egypt or India. Bought a tablecloth of vivid colors with a native character on it.

Went to the beach. Beautiful setting and good body-surfing. Quite a big British colony here so we saw some white women for a change.

Met Harry Green coming back after 16 months of "Over the Hump" work. He flew 69 missions. He's about 20 pounds lighter and says it's pretty tough work between the Japs, the mosquitoes, the weather and the altitude work.

They lost a 54 out of here the other night. It crashed on takeoff, killing 45 people. 36 were men returning to the states after almost two years of over the Hump work. That's really rough!

Jan. 31 - Another day at Accra. Harmattan still going. Swam again. The colonel bought some more Canadian Club and I got a bottle.

Feb. 1 – Visibility still bad, but we left for Kario and Madugiri in Central Africa. Country mostly desert. Got to Kario and had to make instrument approach. In the middle of it they turned off the range and the colonel was really mad. Yelled at Hi, and he got really confused. Finally got in on third pass. Stayed the night as Madugiri was closed in.

Kario is a small post and the village is supposed to be the oldest in Africa. Went into town but didn't get out because of an epidemic of spinal meningitis. Architecture quite remarkable as everything is made from mud brick. Big palace for the chieftain – kids, calves, burros, goats, flies and everything else all sleep in one room. Still very few clothes worn by anyone. Natives all very friendly and all salute with raised fist meaning, "Salute to you, Big Man."

Bought some sandalwood beads and a turtle made from bone. Met a lieutenant who used to be a polo fan in '36 and '37!

Feb. 2 – Long trip across desert country. Took 8:50 of flying. Landed at Khartoum, Anglo-Sudan. As in Accra, they had Red Cross canteens at field with American girls working in them. They looked swell!

Apparently the post is built where old palaces or school buildings used to be. Big rooms, pillars and patios all around.

Picked up a dinner jacket and a filigree silver pin for Nance. Had a milkshake at PX! First milk or ice cream since we left the States.

Flying the Hump

Again had to listen to all sides of a fight between a B-25 crew. Thank Heaven we all get along.

Feb. 3 - Flew to Aden, Arabia, over mountains and desert country. Didn't see any of the pyramids or the Suez Canal. Aden has a big harbor and a ship was sunk by sub just a few hours after we got there. The survivors were pretty sick-looking guys. Went to town but didn't shop. Typhus epidemic.

Reservoirs here were built out of solid volcanic rock terraced out of a mountain and supposedly done by the Queen of Sheba. It's otherwise a rotten town and a rotten post. The natives are unreliable, the climate awful, and the country solid desert.

Feb. 4 - Long flight across Arabia and the Gulf of Arabia to Karachi, India. Landed west into the sun and couldn't see much, but made a pretty damn good landing.

Big post – too late to go into town, but picked up two small ivory elephants and an ivory good luck god at a curio shop on the field

These are the ivory elephants my dad purchased in India. They now reside in my house. (Denise M. Dominick photo)

and went to a show. Ran into Joe Thornton, my former co-pilot, on his way back to the States. He took the ivory figurines with him to mail to Nance. Hope he remembers it. Slept in a tent.

Feb. 5 – Persuaded colonel to stay at Agra so I could see the Taj Mahal! It's just as lovely as the pictures show. Built in 1630 out of solid white marble, inlaid with semi-precious stones as a tomb and a memorial for the sheik's favorite wife! We had to put sandals on over our shoes, as it is holy to the Mohammedans. Couldn't keep them on, and the colonel finally just kicked his ahead of him, to everyone's horror.

Went on to Gaya, a post where there is nothing to entertain one and nothing going on. Red Cross here again but no women working as in the other posts.

Feb. 6 - Arrived in Chabua, India, the delivery point of our plane. Everything's a foot deep in mud. Went to the headquarters for the eastern section and they assigned Randell, Wells, Aicholtz and me to Tezpur, back down in the valley. The C.O.'s have all been changed and the colonel didn't know where to go. Unloaded cargo, gave Brokaw my presents to take back on the C-46 he was navigating back, and flew back to Jorhat to leave the colonel. Unloaded him and his liquor and took off for Tezpur in the dark. Landed at night for the first time since October and got a car to take my stuff to our area. Our new APO is 429 Station 5. Got memo receipts signed for the plane. Everyone's moving to the new area and consequently there was no bedding, no bed nets, no mattresses, no water and no lights. Fell into bed quickly.

Feb. 7 – Signed in at Personnel. Cleared thru Flight Surgeon and went to billeting. Got assigned permanent quarters. Went to Operations, found I will have to make at least 5 trips over Hump and then get 16 hours of transition, mostly instrument

Flying the Hump

This War Department ID card was issued in February 1945. (Image courtesy of Special Collections and Archives, University of Denver)

work, specialized Hump instrument before acting as 1st pilot. May take two months - it makes me sick!

But, they've only lost two planes in the last three months, here and at Jorhat. Without that training they lost 16 ships in the month of January. Losses are pretty high and they aren't saving as many of the crews who try to walk out. Mostly caused by bad icing and more Japs.

Tezpur supposed to be the best post in the valley but the food is very poor. Our magazines accepted with great delight by the guys here. Wrote Nance.

Letter Excerpt

Editor's note: Here is a paragraph or two from this letter to my mother. My dad wrote often, sometimes talking about his life and activities there, but also expressing his deepest love for his wife and children:

"What amazes me the most is not how desolate or forlorn the posts are, but how well-equipped. The Army certainly has done a whale of a job on that. Of course our point of view is different from that of the guys stationed here or there, and the only satisfaction they could derive is that there are darn few posts more lonely than this, with the possible exception of patrolling the Aleutians in a sub chaser....

My only regret in our whole married life is that we haven't (yet) got a daughter who looks just like you. She'd have two older brothers to pester and take care of her, see that she was a good dancer, kept her nails reasonably short, and didn't try to reform too many bums before marrying some mountaineer with shaggy ears.... I have to run again darling – a briefing, not the john. I love you my sweetheart and only hope and pray that more people who can think and act like you develop out of this war to make the world a better place."

Feb. 8 - Spent all day trying to fix up my room. Swiped three seats from plane, some rope and a couple of thermoses. Split bamboo for bed net poles. Went to Supply, got some bedding and a couple of kerosene lamps. Got some lumber and made a table. Swiped some nails to hang things on. Made some stilt legs for chairs. Tried to get an Indian bearer, but no luck. We have no showers here and no running water of any kind. Saw movie.

Feb. 9 - Fixed bamboo poles across room to hang lights on. Swiped a chair for the porch. Went to town. Dirty little Indian village, nothing quaint or pretty about it. Bought some straw mats, a razor, brush and soap for Hig, some 1932 cookies, an Indo-China insignia for my leather jacket, a pail and a wash bowl – the latter "Made in Japan." Got a flag from briefing to put in my jacket to show Chinese I am American and not Japanese, and that a reward would be paid to those helping me. That's in case we have to bail out over the Hump.

Went to another movie. Got a bearer.

Feb. 10 - Told we were on alert for a trip.

Impressions on trip over here: 1) Dullness of long cross-country flights, 2) Tremendous amount of desert we passed over, 3) India is a beautiful country but with the exception of personal because the natives are not friendly, 4) How I miss hot water and running water, 5) Open air movies from Belen to here – much nicer than the movie houses, 6) The dirt the people live in, 7) How friendly the Africans were and how surly the Indians, 8) Tremendous artistic skill in carving, whether of ivory or ebony or plain bone, 9) How high the prices and how poor the food, 10) The number of planes lost per month over the Hump.

The countryside up to the Valley of Assam, where we are, is completely cultivated and yet just southwest of here is supposed to abound with elephants, deer, water buffalo and tigers. I saw what must have been an elephant when we were flying over. To the north and south and east we are ringed in by hills and mountains rising to 23,000 feet. Northwest of us lies Mt. Everest.
Hi and I were both alerted for our first trip – as co-pilots. Called down about 17:00 but trip called off because of weather. Icing and not topped at 25,000 feet. Read and wrote Nance.

Feb. 11 – Went to the APO and made sure my address is correct at HQ. Sent a sandalwood elephant home.

Called to fly at 16:00, co-pilot for Richie. We took off but were called back at Chabua on account of weather.

Alexander S. Dominick

Feb. 12 - Called at 04:00 for flight. Stumbled down to line and took off at about 06:00. Still with Richie. Very thorough and conscientious. He was in 43-B but has about 400 hours on 24's.

Beautiful day – not a cloud. The country up to Chabua is beautiful, and from there on magnificent but overpowering. Much more rugged than Alaska. We flew over to Kunming at about 19,000 feet, on oxygen of course, and back at 18,000. We cleared everything in our path but to the left and right the peaks rose to 20,000 feet. People have bailed out and walked out of there but it looked to me as though if we hit any one of those peaks we would be split up the middle. They are actually knife-edged.

All the first half of the trip the mountains were covered with new-minted snow gleaming in the sunshine, and, except for the very highest peaks, all decked out with evergreens. In between the ridges run rivers of brilliant green surrounded by heavy foliage.

Beyond the halfway point it becomes very evident that the Chinese are the hardest-working people in the world. They have terraced and watered the land and have small villages throughout, usually grouped near the rivers. They must climb 6,000 feet every day merely to till the land. Yunnanyi, about three quarters of the way over, is nestled under Mt. Tali, about 16,000 feet high and on the edge of the lake. It's really beautiful. From Chabua to Fort Hertz, the country is high with thick jungle rising to 14,000 feet and inhabited by the Naga head hunters. At the edge of their domain is the Ft. Hertz valley, running north and south where the Japs have three bases 15 or 20 minutes south: Bhana, Myitkyina and Sumprabum. They come up the valley, shoot down about 10 ships in a couple of months, and then retire for a couple of months. There is no doubt that they could almost stop this route if they wanted to, but either it isn't worth the effort or instead, as most fellows believe, a good third of what we bring to China ends up in Jap hands through Chinese warlords.

Kunming, where we went, is booming with activity. The runway, 6,500 feet long, is at 6,200-foot elevation, and was built completely by hand by Chinese coolies, out of rock crushed by hand. The airport is surrounded by 8,500 foot mountains and I imagine an instrument approach would be pretty rough.

The trip over is about 3½ hours, and about 4½ hours back because of prevailing winds which rise to a velocity of 150 mph. A lot of ships have been lost in the last 3 months – more than an average of one per day, but it's getting better because of better training, because they close the route when there's very bad weather, and because of better radio facilities.

I got some Chinese ivory to add to my collection, and Richie signed it, so that I'm now an official Burma Roadster. I believe that the wear and tear on the nerves is caused by having to be on oxygen for so long rather than the tough flying or Japanese menace, though both those help out of course. Less than a week ago Richie had 4 Zeros on his tail and only got out by having a cloud conveniently near to duck into.

Had a drink on return from trip which I flew from pilot's seat, and to bed. The thing that amazes me most is that information on courses to fly, range frequencies, distances, fields and instrument approaches are all learned by experience, and Operations is only beginning to get a manual out on it. We had no maps, no range cards, nothing but Richie's memory when we took off.

Feb. 13 – Loafed most of the day. As usual slept through breakfast. Long talk, or argument, with Stafford on post-war problems. Some of the boys went to church. Built a table out of half an electrician's cable roller. Wrote a long letter to Nance.

Feb. 14 – Hi and I both had our second trip – mine with Captain Miller – his 69th. He shows the wear and tear on the nerves, being extremely jittery. Went to Chunking. Flew over late afternoon, arriving at night and getting back about 01:00. Japs reported out but didn't see any. Rumors in China that Germany has asked for 36 hours to discuss peace terms. Hope it's true.

Discovered that Sandy Agnew, a cousin of George Agnew who married Lolly Aldridge, is here on post.

It sure gets cold at night over that Hump at 20,000 feet!

Valentine's Day – what a laugh.

Feb. 15 – Another trip. I'm now teamed up with Lt. Nevins, a 2nd Lieutenant, Class 43-A. He is an instructor pilot so I get to fly from left seat. He flies over and lands, I fly back. After the present transition class I'll probably get transition. Got back at 00:30.

Feb. 16 – General Arnold (Maj. General Hap Arnold, Chief of Staff of the Army Air Corps) is coming to give Presidential Citations to the boys who were here in December. Went to town alone and bought a tablecloth, shoe shine equipment, some 2-year-old cookies and some doughnuts. Also bought a really good ivory figurine for Nance. Cost the Indian national debt, but worth it. Movies and to bed. Capt. May started drinking our rum before breakfast, kept it up all day, and when we came back from the show he was passed out on Hi's bed.

Feb. 17 – Waited to be called most of the day. Wrote Nance, Janey and Jack Dent, and Bill Allen. Talked to Capt. Bill Haynie about transition and I'll start next week. I'm 3rd in line.

Started over with Nevins about 20:30 and turned back an hour out when Number 2 prop governor went out and my oxygen wasn't working right. That demand system isn't so hot.

Gorgon, our bearer, said he was leaving, but we got him a new pass and now he's happy again!

Feb. 18 – Parade today, and General Hoag pinned some Presidential Citations of ICW (the India China Wing) on a few guys. The whole unit gets it for work done in December. It's the first time a citation has been given to a "non-combatant" unit and is a pretty good distinction. In order for a unit to earn it, each man is supposed to be engaged in work when he could earn a Distinguished Service Cross. Those joining the unit after December are entitled to wear it also. Seems to be a pretty firm rule now that we get the Air Medal after 150 hours over the Hump and the DFC after 300 hours. Maybe I'll get a medal. Who knows.

Called down for a flight with Nevins. He told me to fly from the left seat, which is pretty good, as I'm not supposed to fly a loaded ship at night into China till after being checked out. Took off and got almost to Chabua and the flight indicator went out. Turned around, came back, and flew over an hour later. Got to Kunming about midnight. Left there about 01:30 and got back here just as dawn was breaking. Some nine hours of flying in all, and we were really tired.

Got paid for January and sent $300 home.

Feb. 19 – Heard today that Captain F.O. Smith lost number 3 engine and then number 4 coming back. Landed at Sookerating, and just barely got in.

Slept and loafed all day.

Feb. 20 – More link-homing on a track. Don't understand their method, which involves higher mathematics but came out OK with my own. Slept and read and wrote Nance.

Feb. 21 - Two days till Mike's birthday. Wish I was with him. Maybe I can send a wire from China in time. Understand we won three houses in Cassino, Italy. At this rate we'll be in Rome by '46.

Still reading "Crescent Carnival." It's good, but long and irritating. People are very spineless at times, myself included.

Went to a movie. Hi is still feeling bad. Don't know what's the matter.

Feb. 22 - Prospective trip to Agra not for me after all though Johnny Nevins went.

Called at 6 AM for link training. My God. Doesn't look as though I'll get to China in time for a wire, and I can't send one from here.

Feb. 23 – More link-homing on a track. Didn't do well at all. Loafed and read and wrote. I was called and asked if I'd defend a prisoner in a court martial case. Agreed.

Feb. 24 – If chosen by my prisoner as counsel I have a tough case. He's been convicted three times in court martials and is being tried for escaping confinement.

Flew to Chunking and back. Hit bad weather and icing coming back. Climbed to 26,000 feet to get over it. Ice cracked off when we let down at Chabua, like hail on a tin roof.

Mike's birthday today, and no wire sent nor mail from Nance.

Feb. 25 - Have been chosen as counsel. Prisoner seems OK, but he has a bad record. Have to plead guilty to escape charges and try to get him off with a light sentence. It will be tough. My hope for jurisdictional issue is out.

Feb. 26 – Hi went to Chabua Hospital to see what's the matter with him.

Got charges and tried to draw up a defense. Not much good.

Found out "my teeth are in trouble if I don't get the gum trouble under control." Baloney. It's under control and the DDS is crummy.

Won at poker.

Feb. 27 – Transition starts next week.

Ordered a tiger cub, a cheetah and a mongoose from an MP sergeant who has a native who is getting him a tiger cub.

Had another talk with the prisoner and the Trial Judge Advocate. The latter said he'd join in a request for transfer and a remission of part of his sentence.

Wrote Nance. Lost at poker.

Feb. 28 - Bud's birthday. Wonder where he is.

Trial took place. Did my best but had no case. The prisoner got the limit: 6 months and 2/3 of pay. No remission of time already served. Transfer request recommended. Discovered that the prisoner had broken out of jail again (not on their court martial charges), and will be tried again in a general court martial at Chabua for that. He'll probably get a Dishonorable Discharge.

Poor guy – he's only 21 and OK if handled right. I sure need experience in trial work. I don't get excited enough, I guess. It was good experience for me, but tough on him.

It seems to me that prison should not be a place to punish guys but a place to rehabilitate them and try to get them so that they'll be useful for more than crooks, giving policemen jobs or chronic guard house men. But that's certainly not the Army way, nor I'm afraid the civilian method yet. Maybe that's a good crusade for me to take up. I've always been interested in it since the course I took, the visit to Sing Sing, and my night in the West Haven jug.

No mail yet, dammit!

Feb. 29 – Talked last night with Stafford for 2 or 3 hours after going to bed on French history, of all things! He has never been to college but has real curiosity. The things that interested him the most are whether or not the French took baths, and what started the Revolution. I'm going to try to get Helen Waddell's "Abelard and Eloise" for him.

Finished most of the trial details today and may still be able to get part of his sentence remitted.

Called for a flight to Chanyi, China tonight. It was beautiful going over but a long trip back because of very strong headwinds (80-100 mph.) Evidently a push is being prepared with Chanyi as backlog for reserves as all ships in the valley have been going in there for the past three or four days. There's been talk of a Japanese offensive using paratroopers to attack Chinese airports. That would really be a disaster.

The Trial Judge Advocate warned me I may be made regular defense counsel. That would be fun.

The Diary
Part 2

Mar. 1 - Slept late as we didn't get in till 5. Wrote Rineharts and Nance, then went to the show.

Mar. 2 - Sent $300 home by P.T.A. Sent cards for forwarding mail to Delhi and Chabua, as I'm getting desperate for some.

Called for flight at 11:30 but didn't get out till 18:30. Beautiful night but strong winds. Went to Chengkung as copilot. I ran out of oxygen on the way back. It was rough as I almost passed out.

Prepared papers for remission of time served in my court martial case.

Missed Melvyn Douglas's show which was here. He is a captain and a Special Services Officer for the District.

Mar. 3 - Read my record and signed it after sleeping late as we didn't get in till 05:30. Played poker and won again.

I start transition next week. Went to the movie.

Mar. 4 – If I remember correctly, this used to be Inauguration Day. Had another Link lesson and a typhoid shot. Just one more bug in me.

Mar. 5 - Made breakfast and went to church. Spent a couple of hours trying to fix a Victrola and only got myself covered in grease.

Ground school started. Everywhere I go, I go to school, dammit!

Wrote a letter to Alsop.

Mar. 6 – Ground school again. Found the showers. Played chess.

What a hard war! Our bearer hasn't shown up in three days and is now officially fired.

Went to movies and wrote Dad and Nance.

Mar. 7 - Called for transition at 05:30. Beautiful morning, but plane out of commission.

Censored mail, wrote family and Jacobson. Latter had three months taken off his sentence by Maj. Gavins who used to run a trucking business and hired ex-convicts. He doesn't believe in hounding people either.

Read "Home is the Hunter" all afternoon and I neither like nor understand it; possibly because I don't understand it. I've never liked the French anyhow as they seem to have very little sense of the proportion of living.

Mar. 8 – Called at 05:00 for transition. Three and a half hours of hard instrument work including homing on a track to and away from a station on the radio compass and loop. Did OK. I

This is a C-87, the type flown by my father and other American pilots on missions "over the hump" in the China-India-Burma Theater of Operations during World War II. (Photo courtesy USAF, via Air Mobility Command Museum, Dover Air Force Base, Delaware)

think. Captain Anderson is really swell as our instructor. Two more hours of ground school in the afternoon. Then, movie, poker and headache. Big day.

To bed at 01:30.

Mar. 9 – Called at 05:00 for a China trip. Went to Chengtu. It's north and farther east than other fields and is China as I pictured it. It's in a valley and there are rice fields as far as can be seen from 18,000 feet. The airport is being built for B-29's, as usual by coolies. There are 100,000 of them and the place looks like an anthill.

They don't move when you come in to land, merely lying down and hoping you don't hit them. Chinese mothers aged about 14 wander around with their kids, and they are so damn cute!

Most of the field is new, but there are some stone administration buildings and Japanese cherry trees blooming. The town, about 5 miles away, has five universities in it so one gets the whole mixture of China, from the Army to the coolies to the educated young boys and girls. The latter are very pretty, and, I understand, partial to Americans, but we never stay longer than an hour so I guess I can't find out!

We have to cross the main Himalayas to get there and it's quite an experience looking up at a mountain from 20,000 feet.

First letter from home. Nance mailed it on February 22nd and numbered it No. 25. None of the other 24 have shown up. It was certainly marvelous to get news but some of it leaves me in the dark as it refers to the other letters. Typical of the Army to get a letter here in two weeks and not to get those mailed almost two months ago.

Mar. 10 – Link – gas drill – haircut, and letter to Nance. Read "Time" to catch up on news, threw a football around, took a shower, played craps, went to the movies, played poker...typical lazy day.

Mar. 11-13 - Nothing new. Busy in the mornings censoring mail. Some poor guys really have their troubles.

Losing steadily at poker – am about even over my whole stay now.

Got two letters from Nance and two from family. Apparently Bud is in Scotland. That should be pretty nice. Wrote Nance, family and the Potters.

Trying to grow a mustache but it's a pretty feeble effort.

Stafford's getting bad and ornery again. The guy's got no sense at all in his relationship with people, or a sense of relative values. Hope he gets transferred to Misamari to fly C-47's, as rumor has it.

Mar. 14-18 – The days go by much the same. The last four days, however, have been pretty active. I completed night transition in 2½ hours and then had a check flight to Kunming. We were weathered in and had to spend the night there. Bought some candy and some flags for our jackets, learned what it said on the flags, and had a long talk with Lt. Brock who used to instruct with me at Turner and is now Operations Officer at Kunming.

Had a good trip back with only one hour of instrument work and landed on three engines. I'm now a Class 2 pilot. After 5 trips I'll be a Class 1. They sure are cautious here. When I got back I found a letter from Hi Randell. Apparently the poor guy has a spinal tumor, and I spent all day yesterday and today packing his stuff and sending it to the Calcutta Hospital.

No mail. Some interesting theories – there is an amphitheater, a valley in the 17,000-foot mountains, about 5 miles long. The cultivation is almost western in appearance, foliage grows all over, and on the side of the mountain is an orderly town with a huge gold-roofed temple to one side. It's almost a replica of "Lost Horizon."

There is one mountain we pass near on the way to Chengtu which seems about 29,000 feet high. The Tibetans claim there is one further in that's 35,000 feet, a good 6,000 feet higher than Everest.

Another story is that there is a race of white people living in the center of unsurveyed Tibet, descendants of Alexander the Great's army!

In one valley on the way to Chengtu live the Lolo's, a tribe that has declared war on Chinese, Americans, Japanese, Tibetans, British – everyone except the Lolo's. They are head hunters and practice the art of shrinking their enemy's heads to about the size of an apple and preserving them that way. If you go down there it's rough.

Capt. Haynie was shot at by Zeros a couple of days ago, and Jorhat lost another C-87.

Mar. 19 – Supposed to take my first flight as pilot but I felt horrible so I went on DNIF (Duty Not Including Flying.) Apperson and Stafford went to rest camp. What a laugh.

Mar. 20 - I still have a cold but felt better, so I got myself off DNIF and went on a flight to Chengtu. Desaussure was my co-pilot. It was a good trip – navigation was good and the landings fair. We got back about 22:00, and on the way to our area found an Indian guard shot. Covered with blood, but unless the ride in a truck to the hospital gets him, he should be OK. He was shot in the leg. Don't know by whom, or when, but I couldn't see how he could've shot himself from the position of the wound. It was really bloody!

Mar. 21 - Back on DNIF, as I expected. Nursed my cold, wrote letters, read and went to the show. Got my name on the list for rest camp in a few days.

The guard died. No one ever found out how it was done.

Mar. 22-26 – Rest Camp: The camp, about an hour and a half drive from the field, is on the edge of the Bearney River, in the low hills northeast of the field.

(Editor's note: "Bearney" is what Dad spelled out, but I can find no reference to a Bearney River. The closest river I can find that matches his description is the Brahmaputra.)

The river is clear, cold and fast, with strong rapids as far as we navigated. Behind the camp is jungle, with all the jungle color and all its strange noises. The whole place is a reserve, so that after making extensive preparations for hunting, the C.O. had to make us leave all guns behind. Apparently the British, bless them, had heard of the three deer the other boys had shot and were scared we'd shoot all the game. Three deer in a month – my God.

Capt. (Doc) Wade and I roamed down the river bank in the jungle the first day and put up three jungle chickens. (They look like big bantam roosters with the same brilliant plumage.) We saw lots of cat tracks and came upon one fresh elephant trail. Some of the other boys went upriver in the truck and rode down the rapids in our yellow life rafts and saw a bear and some otters.

The next day we hung around camp a while, and then Vander-Poel, Galloway and I went upstream through the jungle. Saw nothing but some jungle cocks again, but came on very fresh elephant tracks. Apparently four or five of them had been through no more than ½ hour ahead of us. They had crossed over onto an island on the other side of the river so we couldn't follow.

It rained that afternoon and night and the next morning. Having shot nothing, we were living on weenies and fried dough balls. That afternoon, we took three boats about an hour upriver by truck, then rode the rapids down to camp and hunted too, as a few of us had brought guns anyhow. VanderPoel and I succeeded in getting sopping wet, seeing some beautiful country and having a swell time, but no game.

The river branches all over and then meets up again above camp so you go alone down fast water through thick jungle, with monkeys chattering and rushing through the treetops, jungle cocks crowing, and every now and then some strange roar. Then around a corner the whole place will open up in sandbars and marsh. Perfect deer country, but no deer!

Van, Capt. Guyton, Fluhr and I got up at 5 the next morning and came down again, but no luck. Guyton killed a porcupine and we saw a fawn or a variety of small deer no bigger than an Irish terrier, but we didn't shoot. The birds were brilliantly colored. One I saw when I was out in the jungle alone was about the size of a pileated woodpecker, with the coloring and bill of a toucan. Another was a brilliant baby blue when he flew, but streaked with red and yellow when perching.

But the jungle is no picnic. The ferns grow 7 feet tall. They are lovely, but on the back of them are thorns like razors about ½ inch long. And the ticks and leeches are terrific – I picked 40 leeches off me in less than an hour. When you stand still you can see them inching over the ground and onto your boots, and if you have a scratch they head right for it. They don't hurt, but they leave wounds that won't stop bleeding, and once they're on only a lit cigarette will unclamp them. The only way I could stop my legs from bleeding was to stand in the icy river, and even that wasn't too sure. What they didn't do, the sand fleas, mosquitoes, flies and ticks finished off, so that now I'm a mass of cuts, scratches and bites.

The natives have heard of the rafts we have, so they came to the opposite bank from all over to be ferried across. One night the Doflers came – they are a Tibetan border tribe of "civilized" headhunters, far better-looking than the Indians, and similar to the Gurkhas. They wear an old sheet of some kind combined into a loin cloth, and have knives and bows and arrows for weapons. The Headman is really the Head Man. He tells the rest what they can sell and for what price, and what to do. Fluhr and I managed to buy two of their big knives from them, the first ones they had ever sold! I also got a little knife and a set of tiger teeth one kid was wearing around his neck as an amulet.

They had planned to stay the night behind our camp, but after a half-hour when we were all gathered around a campfire, asking questions through our Indian interpreters, they got mad, and each taking an ember from the fire to ward off evil spirits and animals, they walked off into the night. The Headman was pretty impressive in his control – no one would sell without his OK. One of them didn't trust the raft, as every time he put his foot into it, it gave way, and he could see how the water flowed up around the edges. He would put his foot in and then back off. It happened twice and then the chief barked. I don't know what he said but the guy jumped into the boat immediately and never moved from there over to the other side. Their women should be lovely if they look like the men. They are more yellow than black, and any one of the men, with a dress and some make-up could pass as a good-looking girl – good-looking for here, I mean.

Sunday night we came back and were treated to a show by Paulette Goddard, Bill Gargan, Wynne Dennis and Andi Ardani; the latter, an accordion player, stole the show. But the whole thing was good and very funny.

Apperson has a Chinese water pipe he got at Chengtu. I'll have to try for that myself.

Mar. 27 – Bought stuff from the rations at the PX. Got off DNIF. Played and won at chess. Rained out of movie and wrote Nance.

Mar. 28 – Supposed to be O.D. (Officer of the Day), but got called for a flight at 05:00. Took off and was about to light a cigarette when I smelled gas. I investigated and discovered one of 100 octane gas drums pouring gasoline all over the cabin. Landed at Jorhat and had it fixed. Lucky to get it before we got to altitude and the fumes blew us up. Had Lt. R.O. Smith as co-pilot. He's just over and about to begin transition, so I let him fly back. Wind blew us off course over the overcast at 23,000 feet and wound up just topping a snow-capped peak. It was really high. Yesterday the Japs tried to bomb Sookerating and lost 29 out of 36 ships definitely and 6 probables. One Jap tried to attack a formation of 9 '51's all by himself and was blown to bits like a Buck Rogers ray gun. Had another red alert at Chabua today but nothing doing.

Mar. 29 – The Japs have captured some British bases in India, about 150 miles south of here – near Shillong, so we aren't entirely victorious – we may have some raids here now.

Called for another flight, but because I'm still a Class 2 pilot and the ship not being ready before 14:00 I didn't get off.

Got my haircut and wrote Aunt Helen. Went to show. AA batteries started practicing and our own dumb Special Services Officer figured it was an alert and called one on his own initiative. What a farce!

Chengtu is fully supplied now, so we're all going to Yanghai. It's a tough field, elevation 6,500 feet. We've filled Kunming, Chang-kung, Chanyi, Chengtu – and now we're starting on Yanghai. After that they'll have to start new bases or we'll have to start over again.

Editor's note: The Aunt Helen my dad refers to Helen Smith, wife of my great uncle, US Senator H. Alexander Smith (R-NJ). Uncle Axe, as we called him, was good friends with Dwight

Eisenhower and arranged a meeting between him and my dad when Ike and his wife, Mamie, were in Denver at their summer White House. Mamie was from Colorado. This is how my dad got into politics.

Mar. 30 – Called at 04:00, but air freight didn't get the ship loaded till 10. I was plenty mad. Got a trip to Chengtu. Weather was horrible. Flew two and a half hours on instrument by D.R., (Dead Reckoning) and hit the checkpoint right on the nose. What a relief. We had a snow storm, ice, rain, and strong winds. We even had snow in the cockpit. At Chengtu I got a silver Chinese water pipe for about 9 rupees, and a copper Chinese coin for a cigarette. They are both worth having as souvenirs. Came back on instruments and got St. Elmo's fire all over the plane. Flew through two thunderstorms from necessity not choice, and then had trouble finding the field as our radio compass needles were thrown off by electrical storms and the field was socked in. Really rough trip and a forerunner of monsoon weather.

I now have over 100 hours flying over the Hump. In the old days they got the DFC for that! Ran into Lex Durham, whom I haven't seen since he went to single-engine advanced school in June of '42. He's with A.S.C. on this field. That's going to be swell. I might even be able to persuade him to check me out in a P-40.

Mar. 31 – Rested and relaxed. Got a note from Hi Randel. He expects to leave for the States on April 5th. Got paid, sent $150 home, won 300 rupees at dice and lost 150 at poker. One of the pilots here drowned in the rapids at Rest Camp. Apparently he couldn't swim and was weighted down with 3 .45-caliber pistols and a carbine! It's very ironical. He survived a very bad C-46 crash, flew a lot over the Hump, and he died that way.

Apr. 1 – Lazy day and very unlucky gambling. Wonder I didn't break my leg getting out of bed! Another crash – a colonel in a

B-25. Pure pilot error, but as he is a colonel it will undoubtedly be called mechanical failure. General Wingate was also killed in a crash today. Bad loss, as he's been directing paratroop operations in Burma.

Apr. 2 – Another lazy day but won some of the rupees I lost yesterday. Had a swell letter from Nance and went to church. The Japs are encircling Imphal in India, about 150 miles southeast of here. Apparently it's a counterattack against the drive in Burma and they are doing too damn well. They are only 100 miles from Jorhat just up the line from here. Heard from the colonel who wants his dough for the peanuts and from Hi who leaves in a week with his First Lieutenancy! Wonder how he worked that.

Apr. 3 – Flight to Kunming and back – beautiful weather on top of overcast at 19,000 feet. The Japs have cut the Manipur Road connecting with the Chabua rig. They are about to cut off the latter and that will end supplies by any to all stations east of here. They are now only 35 miles from Jorhat, about 70 from here, and are 3 divisions strong encircling Imphal.

Starting tomorrow we take the cargo to Kunming, unload, go to Yunnanyi and take on a load of Chinese troops and bring them to Sookerating. They are supposed to fight when they get there, but I don't see how, after being carried over the Hump **with no oxygen**. It's a rough assignment for them and us. Maybe if that doesn't stop the Japs they'll let us attack in C-87's with Tommy guns! More fun.

Swell letter from Dad today. Very philosophical and very good too. Somamial (our bearer) is all excited because Stafford told him we might take him to America. Stafford should really be taught a good lesson some day.

Apr. 4 – No news on Jap advance. Read, showered, shaved off mustache and went to show. Sent. Col. Estelle his 100 rupees.

Stafford's in trouble again. He refused to go on a flight last night – and refused four times! No reason, except he was sleeping. Field got recommended by HQ for record number of trips on March 29-30. We flew 34 trips with 24 planes. Pretty good.

Took a 64 Physical. Had trouble with the eye chart and depth perception. Captain Rossi gave me ten tries before I could get it. My old system wouldn't work because the right stick was bigger. Then my right eye read only 20/30. Apparently that's enough now. Anyhow when he asked me if I had glasses with me and I said yes, he changed it to 20/20 and said OK. Lucky I made friends with him before!

Apr. 5 – Read. Lost money at gin rummy. Went to show. Got a letter from Jacobsen, my "client," thanking me and saying everything is going OK.

Apr. 6 – Called at 04:00. Had Young again as copilot. Flew to Chengkung through some of the worst turbulence and light snow. Ordered from Chengkung to Yunnanyi to pick up a load of Chinese troops. Yunnanyi is 6,500 feet and completely surrounded by hills up to 10,000 feet. It's hard to get into and even harder to get out of. The troops, ranging in age from 16 to 60, were packed into the waist of the ship, and we flew back over the Hump to Sookerating in the valley. I stayed as low as I dared, 18-20,000 feet but with no oxygen for them, with most of them scared and sick, it was rough. Not one of them had a chute, and if anything had happened it would have meant bailing out and leaving them to crash, a horrible idea.

At Sookerating they were packed like cattle into trucks and were taken right off to a staging area. I understand we're bringing over at least 1,200 troops a day and they'll fight the Japs advancing north of Imphal. Came back from Sookerating through three thunderstorms, terrific rain, spots of hail and black as a nigger on a dark night. Got in really tired at 22:00 and found two letters from Nance and one from Dad.

Just a week ago the Japs shot up two 46's. One from Chabua crashed with the whole crew, and one from Jorhat flew back riddled with bullet holes – with the copilot and crew chief pretty badly wounded. It's a rough trip across the old Hump.

Apr. 7 – Got up late. Got my beer and candy ration. Loafed, read and wrote. No mail.

Apr. 8 – Called at 03:00. Waited till 9:30 before plane finally OK. Flew into Yanghai for the first time. Had about a 50 mph crosswind and very turbulent. These Chinese fields certainly present obstacles of all kinds. The country around Yanghai, brown with rolling hills, with temperate zone wild flowers, looks like Alberta, Canada. There should be game all over but I guess there are too many Chinese. Had about 100 mph headwind coming back. That really makes it rough.

Apr. 9 – Easter Sunday! Went to church in the morning and read and wrote all afternoon. Played gin rummy and won for a change! No mail. Japs still attacking north of Imphal but apparently not getting much closer to Jorhat.

Apr. 10 – Called at 07:00. Flew to Chunking, and from there to Yunnanyi to pick up Chinese soldiers again. We were just taxiing out to take off when the tower told us, "There's an alert! Goose it!" We swung out and started off, setting superchargers as we went and not bothering to check the mags. The flaps and everything we set as we went. Got off the field, which is rough at best, and swung out south looking for passes in the mountains as I didn't dare circle the field to get altitude. Finally swung back past the field about 7 miles west and heard the tower say, "3 Japs over the field!" Everybody was told to go to Lijiang and then the field went off the air for about an hour. Couldn't see any bombs drop but it wasn't more than 4 minutes from when we took off to when the Japs were there!

Trouble with Number 3 engine at Sookerating but unloaded the Chinese soldiers, who as usual had been sick all over everything, and came back. Had enough excitement for one day. Again no mail. Evidently the priority has been changed from #1 to #3 and it's being held up.

The Matterhorn Project boys, all my friends, are due to go home in a couple of days. Two of them just came down with malaria. That's really rough luck.

Editor's note: The Matterhorn Project was suggested by General Joseph Stilwell at the Trident Conference of Allied leaders in May 1943. The plan was to use the new B-29s, based in India, to launch bombing attacks against Japan. The Project was under the direct command of the Joint Chiefs, with General H.H. Arnold, the Chief of the Army Air Corps, as its Executive Director.

Apr. 11 – Called again right after breakfast. Went to Kunming. The ship wouldn't climb, and there were thunderstorms all over the place, but otherwise OK. Lots of guys calling for bearings as they were "uncertain of their position!"

No mail – dammit! Captain Haynie, our Chief Pilot, and check pilot got completely lost and ended up way south in a field near Bengal Bay after flying for 6½ hours. The British were firing antiaircraft shells at him, and sent up night interceptors etc. because the ship's I.F.F. (Identification, Friend or Foe) wasn't on. Haynie didn't know any of this till later, on the ground. He sure can embroider a story. Lost what little respect the rest of us had for him on that boner.

Apr. 12 – Lazy day. Pitched horseshoes, played gin rummy, slept, got a smallpox shot.

Apr. 13 – Another lazy day but no mail yet. The boys are beginning to get mad over that. Lost heavily at gin rummy.

Apr. 14 – Up at 3 AM for flight. Went to Chengtu. The radio compass froze on me but checked with null and we flew over OK. Made a beautiful landing for a change! Came back the direct route across Tibet and it was beautiful and awe-inspiring. Mountains at least 23,000 feet high and higher in the north. Some of the boys who have been blown north off course claim they were flying on top of 30,000-foot overcast and that mountains were also sticking up higher than 5,000 feet – that makes Everest a baby!

Mail at last! Nance and Dad. Wahoo. Rained out of show.

Apr. 15 – Restful day again. Read and wrote and won at gin rummy again. Jap advance patrols have been sighted only 15 miles from Jorhat and all the boys there are alerted and carry machine guns. We may be used as ground troops yet. If they get Jorhat and the railway, the whole valley east of here will be cut off except by air. That would put the boys in China in a tough spot too, as most of our bases for supplying cargo by air would be gone. But the British are their usual unruffled self-complacent dull selves.

Apr. 16 – Restful morning reading. Expected to be called but no go. Heard that a British field just east of Sookerating had been almost eliminated by Jap bombing – apparently in support of the drive on Kohima and Jorhat. But the field was mostly used as an air emergency base and temporary "peashooter" field. Wrote and won at hearts.

Editor's note: The peashooter referred to here was the Boeing P-26.

Apr. 17 – Went to a very good intelligence summary and lecture on walking out of the Hump. Apparently the Japs have 3 divisions in the drive on the valley – one they are using to bottle up the British forces at Imphal, and they don't particularly care about capturing the place. The other two are further north, one driving on the Manipur Road which they have blocked at one point and cut off at Kohima. These troops are driving on to Dimapur, the junction of the road and the Calcutta-Chabua railway. If they get Dimapur, the east end of the valley will be cut off from supplies except by the Brahmaputra River, which is very low now. This division would then apparently advance north to Jorhat and cut off the Brahmaputra line. The other is bypassing Dimapur to the north and south, apparently aiding in its capture and heading toward us at Tezpur to cut the west railway here. The Hump stuff was the usual.

Got called out to deadhead to Yunnan to pick up a cripple (plane) and bring her back. Flew over at 23,000 and almost froze. The plane of course not ready so we spent the night. Went to town, a dirty mud village swarming with grinning Chinese kids no bigger than maggots all yelling "ting hao" at us, meaning OK. One old woman brought her baby, who couldn't have been more than a year old, up to me, raised his hand for him, stuck up his thumb, mumbled something, and the baby grinned and squeaked "ting hao." Had dinner at a Chinese restaurant – soup, pork cutlets and coffee – for $150 Chinese, about $1.75 American. The countryside is beautiful, a valley 6,500 feet up and surrounded by 13,000-foot mountains – and only ½ hour from the Japs. Went to bed, and the pillow and mattress were so dusty I got hay fever all night.

Apr. 18 – Spent the morning test hopping the plane with a new Number 3 engine – oil pressure low and a leak in the dome on the prop. Finally fixed and flew back at 22,000 feet, ducking cumulus built up to 32,000 feet at least. Heard over a French broadcast from Saigon that the Japs are only 6 miles from Dimapur in force. Expect to get a night check and be Class 1 tomorrow night, damn it. Let the Crew Chief fly the plane for forty-five minutes. He has some 800 hours and has applied to be a service pilot but no results yet. A lot better than the copilot I had!

Apr. 19-22 – Spent half a lazy day and then got orders appointing me defense counsel in a case of two men found sleeping on guard. Discovered that they were being charged as watchmen before a special court instead of guards before a general court martial. Both men were found at the same post, our most important, and sleeping side by side. Had trial on the 21st and the 22nd, and by a miracle I almost had the men acquitted. They argued over a motion to dismiss for an hour, decided against me and when declared guilty they only got 4-month fines, the maximum being 6 months' confinement at hard labor and 6 months fine of 2/3rds of their pay. The cases ran smoother and I believe I did a better job – certainly a better job than I expected. Finished up by winning back the 200 rupees I had lost at gin rummy. All very satisfactory.

Apr. 23 – Called early and went to Chengtu. Apperson along as copilot. Good trip and interesting as again I went over the northern "mountainous" route. Got home to a letter from Dad, one from Bill Allen telling me of his engagement to Adaline, and one from Nance, best of all. Guess I'm getting homesick.

Apr. 24 – Called about noon for a flight to Chanyi with Martini. The ship apparently was balanced wrong or the ships of that series are built differently so that they can't carry the load. We couldn't indicate more than 153. Took quite a while to get there and then landed on grass. Back at 01:30. Weather good for a change.

Apr. 25-27 – Sat around and relaxed. Wrote Nance a couple of letters. Played gin rummy and hearts and for a change I'm winning. Got a new roommate from Chabua, a boy by the name of Johnson. He's been here for four months and only has two trips. Apparently Chabua is really horrible. The new C.O., a snake pilot, has them doing drills and calisthenics in this heat! Johnson's married and has a kid in the oven and expected next week. He's also an artist of sorts and specializes in Petty and Vargas drawings, so our basha should be well decorated. Apparently the Matterhorn guys are going home on the 1st and their ships are being moved to Jorhat. Afraid it will have us short of planes. Thank Heaven Brise is staying as all my other friends are in the Matterhorn group.

Apr. 28 – Read February Reader's Digest and plays by Odets and Behrman. Wrote family and explored the country around the camp. It's extremely dull! Called for transition. Flew, had one bad landing, and then on the next takeoff our Number 1 engine caught fire and was feathered. Went around and greased one in and everything was OK. Passed and saved some time. Have a route check and then will be Class 1.

Apr. 29 – Loafed, played cards, and had an object lesson in how to draw. Kuhlman's roommate, also a Lt. Johnson, used to work for Disney and Vargas and can do crayon work as well as airbrush. He does portraits in about 15 minutes and they are really good.

Apr. 30 – Got paid all the money the boys owe me. Have won about 1,000 rupees, and when I get paid will send $150 home. The planter's deal screwed up as they called us with no warning and Brise is in Calcutta with the B-17 talking to Gen. Hardin. The Matterhorn guys leave tomorrow and we threw a big party. I'll sure hate to see them go. Apperson, Desaussure, Henley, Grubb, Wade, Hunter, Kuhlman, Huddleston, Joe, Dwyer – all the men I knew best. Charteris and I argued all night and then I carried him to bed.

The Diary
Part 3

May 1 – The boys left today. Henley and Apperson have Nancy's address and have promised to call. Henley is taking the water pipe with him. Got paid and sent $150 home. Got called for a flight but the Hump was closed, thank Heaven. I hadn't recovered from the party last night.

May 2 – Called for a flight to Yunnanyi. The weather was horrible – rain, ice, snow, hail... No radio till we got there. Made procedure turnaround on range and came in. Heller, who took off before me got severe ice and was lost for a long while. We left shortly on our way home and had Number 2 engine start to burn up and Hump close at the same time. Feathered Number 2 and went back to Yunnanyi for a 3-engine landing. Spent the night while sneezing, fighting off fleas, and freezing. China is pretty but Lord how it stinks!

May 3 – Oil cooler changed. Took off and flew on instruments all the way back. Thunderstorms, rain, ice and snow. Ceiling about 500 feet back here. Slept, lost 500 rupees playing craps, wrote Nance and won at gin rummy.

May 4 – Lost the rest of my rupees at craps and finally decided it's no way to win money. Read, and wrote Bill Allen on his engagement to Adaline.

May 5 – Slept late. Coffee shop opened today and we can now get coffee and cake at odd hours. It's run as a Red Cross project but operated by G.I.s so there are no frills to it.

May 6 – Flew over to Yunnanyi. Bad trip. Going over I guessed wrong and tried to climb over banked weather on the Salween River. I went into it at 19,000 feet and was still in it at 23,000 with heavy turbulence and ice. Got past the main part of the Hump and dived down, getting under it at about 17,000. And coming back was worse.

They closed the Hump to all but us, and we proceeded in good shape to just short of the first ridge. Thunderstorms were massed there but we squeaked through a hole. There were storms all around and the radio compasses kept homing on the storms. I got what I thought was a wing tip on Chabua and turned for Jorhat not at all worried. We never did get a fix on Jorhat so I turned when I estimated it and headed for Tezpur where the weather was supposedly good.

It was very black, partly overcast and in layers. We let down slowly, but at 6,000 feet, where Tezpur should have been, we saw nothing and could get no radio reception because of the storms. So I flew around a box course and still couldn't find it. After ½ hour I called for a bearing. At the end of an hour following the bearings we were no better off. Finally, I got a null on the radio for a couple seconds and so I followed that in, climbing like mad for fear I was wrong – that some of the clouds would have rocks in them.

We were sure glad to see the field. Took us 4:40 for a 2:40 trip and we knew we were within 15 minutes of the field all the time.

May 7-8 – Sat around resting all day and at 20:30 got called for my Class 1 check to China. We had the worst weather imaginable, taking off in a blinding rain and running into the turbulence of a thunderstorm while just off the ground. The valley was bad all the way and we hit heavy icing at Ft. Hertz and Salween areas. Got to China at 03:30. Hump closed. Went to get coffee and found the Chinese cook asleep on a hard bench using a can of condensed milk for a pillow. So I lay down for an hour and was then called. Halfway back the Hump was closed again but we came back anyhow. Really tired. Slept all afternoon, saw the movie and then wrote Nance.

May 9 – Wrote Hi Randel who is in bad shape. Can't walk and has to have someone shave him and write for him. He's in a hospital at Coral Gables now with some kind of viral disease the docs don't understand! Wrote Adaline on her engagement to Bill Allen and wrote Bill Everdell. Had a lesson on drawing and perspective from Johnson who used to do airbrush work at the Disney Studios. It's hotter than hell and no relief in sight.

May 10 – Called last night but didn't get off until early this morning. Had the tanker and she really moves gas. All her bomb bay is filled with fuel tanks. We carry it over that way instead of in drums as in the 87's, but it takes so long to unload her that an 87 can make one and a half trips to our one and even up the amount of gas delivered. The tanker is also pretty bad in rough weather with gas slopping over like a ship with a shifting load. Had a good trip but again no sleep.

May 11 – Got another package from home. Pate de foie gras, orange crystals, etc. This was mailed on Feb. 3rd. Won some rupees at gin rummy.

May 12 – Called early and flew to Chanyi. This night flying is getting rough on me. Again had no sleep. Apparently Stillwell's troops are doing well and already there are rumors that we may be moved near Calcutta or down to Ceylon. Had a good trip but am getting pretty tired!

May 13 – Another package from Nance. More pate, some boned turkey and some orange crystals. A letter from Dad suggesting I buttonhole the C.O. and ask about my promotion. I got next to him at the dice table and lost all the rest of my rupees but that's all!

Got called out again early in the evening and got back about 2:30 AM. No sleep. Relaxed and wrote Nance. Got called again at 08:00 but refused to go. Three days with no sleep after 5 out of 7 days of flying at night is too much. I got mad and told everyone off at Operations. Went to bed for a good sleep for a change.

May 14 – Mother's Day. Went to church. Got called for a flight at noon and got off at about 4 PM. Went to Chanyi again. Good trip over. Apparently we have a field only some 100 miles or less from the Chinese coast. They took it back from the Japs, who could take it back any time they wanted to but apparently it isn't worth the effort. I gather we use it for weather and reconnaissance reports. We've already lost one of the three B-29's at Chengtu to enemy action. The last we heard it was being attacked by ten Zeros over the Hump.

Also got a new slant on the Chinese last night from an officer who has been in India and China. He prefers the Indians – the Chinese smell more, and they certainly do! You can smell some of them from ½ a mile. They steal anything left around, they delight in torturing animals. They started skinning a dog without killing him, and he escaped and ran around with his hind quarters all skinned out. They dipped a rat in gasoline, put a match to it and howled with glee while the rat raced around and burned up. The women in the poor class are 90% afflicted with venereal disease of all sorts, many of them hereditary. They never leave you alone in quiet and the Chiang Kai Shek government can't

This is my dad's hand-written list of aircraft he flew and the dates. (Image courtesy of Special Collections and Archives, University of Denver)

even keep down the bandits who have already started raids on two of our fields, one at Chengtu and the other at Chanyi. They leave the Americans alone now as a result of those two.

Trip back was good as far as the valley. It was one mass of thunderstorms. Stayed at 24,000 feet until we were over the field, and then spiraled down between three storms. Landed in hard rain and terrific thunderstorm display and very heavy crosswinds. Almost missed the runway.

Discovered I am an instructor again. I'm going to be a check pilot over the Hump. They would pick now just when I'm having a bad spell of flying! It should help my promotion along some and I'll get longer trips, and I can split more of the flying. I hope there isn't too much night work.

May 15 – Loafed most of the day and then had transition to see whether I knew aerial null work for check pilot work. It went fairly well.

May 16 – No mail for the last few days. Got called at noon for a flight and checked Baines, who had previously ridden as my copilot and who was with me when I fell asleep! Had smooth instrument weather and a let down at Chanyi. Broke through below our minimum but still had 200 or 300 feet over the mountain tops. Baines did a fair job but seems nervous, and when I cut an outboard engine on his landing back here he really sweated it out. He still needs experience in the plane.

Got back in time for a swell show: Lifeboat.

May 17 – Heard that I've been made President of the Officers Club. How silly! I know nothing about it, and there's probably a lot of work associated with it. Japs were out in force in the morning, attacking Shinbwiyang, Chabua, and Mohanbari, but I didn't hear the results. Got called for a flight at about 17:00, but didn't get off till 20:00. Good trip to Kunming, but a horrible old plane.

May 18 – Coming back in the early hours this morning we ran into a storm and had the biggest display of St. Elmo's Fire I've ever experienced. The props had a perfect halo around them, the pitot tubes were green arrows in the night, and it played all over the windows, like ghostly luminous fingers trying to get in. It was really eerie. Got back at 05:00 and was in bed by 06:00. Slept until 10, but by then it was too hot. 95 degrees already, and it's like that every day! Arranged to go to the British Tea Planters on Saturday. I've put in some 80 Hump hours already this month, not to mention local flying, so a week off should do me good.

Heard I have a lot of cases coming up to defend which will be dillies, including the G.I. up for manslaughter for shooting the Indian guard.

Played volleyball and am dead. To bed early. Probably fly early tomorrow morning.

Got a letter from Nance, the first in several days. Apparently everybody's sick again – I don't like it as it makes two months now that there has been continual sickness.

May 19 – Leaving tomorrow for the Planters, so I took the day off. Played volleyball, read and packed.

May 20-29 – Brise, Hamilton, Markley, Murray, Richie and I, along with about 5 others I didn't know, all piled into trucks and drove northeast about 20-50 miles to the various tea plantations. We crossed the Borelli River on a native ferry made of 2x4 logs stretched across two dugout canoes, with a small engine in our canoe and two boys with big sweeps as wheelmen. The current was fast but they had it down to a science and maneuvered both across at once. The roads were bad and none of us knew what we were in for so we didn't feel too happy, but arrival at the first point, the Lightbody's, where Richie and Murray are staying, changed all that. Horn and Markley went on to the Worcester's, and Harry and I to the Barry's.

All the spots are known as bungalows, but "be it ever so humble," there's no place smaller than a mansion. The Barry's place was built out of stone and stucco, two stories with a wide porch running all around the lower floor, a thatched roof with overhanging eaves and steel pillars – a combination of Southern plantation, Chinese pagoda and skyscraper architecture, but useful to keep it cool (high ceilings), dry and earthquake-proof.

The house was completely surrounded by a wide green lawn, shaded by big gum and golden mohr trees, the latter covered with their beautiful blooms and edged with English and Indian flower gardens. In peacetime there had been two grass tennis courts, but the Barrys had stopped playing and turned one into a putting green and the other into a badminton court. In the distance were the barrier hills. The home itself was very comfortably- and well-furnished, our bedroom alone being big enough to get lost in, and of course the bearers seemed to be swarming around every corner but never underfoot.

Mr. Barry (Abie), a man of about 45, has been out here since the last war. Apparently he couldn't get his job as an engineer back when he was demobilized, his family would have nothing to do with him because he was Irish and fought with the British, and so he grabbed the first job he could get. He came out as Assistant Manager of one of the gardens and worked his way up to become Superintendent of three gardens, and will probably be asked to be a director of the agency in Calcutta.

Mrs. Barry (Marion), is about 33, very attractive in an English way, very efficient in her household, and slowly is getting heartily tired of tea and the Assam Valley. Both of them had great senses of humor and we kidded back and forth about everything from Lifebuoy soap to British politics and had a marvelous time. We had hot baths, inner-spring mattresses, fresh meat and of course tea at every hour and on all occasions. Marion even had ice tea made for us.

The tea business is a really tight monopoly run almost entirely by a couple of holding companies in London. These holding companies have agencies in Calcutta, Bombay, Darjeeling, etc., and each agency controls several companies. The Barrys' agency had three companies, one of which he was Superintendent of, the Biswanath, which has three gardens. The big money, of course, is back in London with the holding companies, but the men in the agencies also coin it as do the Directors of the different companies. The men actually running the gardens, the ones we knew, live very comfortably but would have a rough time saving enough to go home and retire on.

They have a small golf and tennis club for the planters, and have open days twice a week, Wednesdays and Sundays, when they all gather to play billiards, or golf or tennis, or drink and dance a little, but even with us all there to liven it up somewhat, we all went home again by 11 PM.

Marion and I beat Harry and Abie both times we played, me distinguishing myself by making two birdies, an eagle and several pars in between my customary 8s and 9s. Once I played tennis, once badminton, and the rest of the time relaxed and read, or slept or ate or talked. Harry and I would stagger out of bed around 10:30 and wander down to a delicious breakfast of eggs or fish cooked in special sauces, and then two hours later have a glass of tea and then lunch at 1:00 or 1:30. After lunch everyone went to bed till 4:30, when tiffin was served. Tea, cookies, cakes, laughter and dogs all jumbled into one memory. After tiffin came the activity to go on for the day, and dinner was served after cocktails anytime from 7:30 to 11:30 PM. What a life!
But good things always seem to come to an end, and we all struggled back on the 29th, carrying parcels of tea and lychee nuts, and promising to return by air and buzz the place and bombard them with cigarettes.

Murray and Richie had been on an elephant ride, and I had a promise from Mr. Pisey to go hunting unclassified rhinos in Tibet. He was the head of the "V Force" that probably saved Assam when the Japs took over Burma.

(Editor's note: Reading the history of the V Force, it's clear that Mr. Pisey was not actually the head of the effort – most likely he was one of the local commanders.)

5 men, planters living in Assam, volunteered to raise a native force and harass the Japs. Pisey was in charge of the other four, a group of 200 Ghurka soldiers donated by the army and 300 Naga hillsmen recruited when they got there. They lived off of, fought with and in the jungle for months at a time, and even pushed patrols as far south as Myitkyina. The Chinese were supposed to be helping them but spent most of the time not showing up. Once a Chinese Major held up the colonel and even fired shots at him while they swiped the boots parachuted to them by the British. My opinion of the Chinese as honorable people and good fighting men is dropping every day.

Found five letters from Nance, one from Aunt Helen, one from Bill Allen, two from Dad, and four envelopes with airmail stationery from Marmie. Thank Heaven Nance and the kids seem to be getting well. Wrote Nance.

May 30 – Wrote another letter and played chess.

Called for a flight at 20:00 to check Lofland. Went to the plane and found that the gas crew had dropped a pencil in the Number 4 gas tank, so I argued 588 from another crew and we took off about 22:15. About 50 minutes out, after going through a thunderstorm, I noticed the Number 4 cylinder head temperature was low. I closed the cowl flap but it didn't move so I figured the instrument was out. 15 minutes later the Number 4 oil temperature started to go up, so I watched for trouble, and just as we went over the main Hump at 21,000 feet, the Number 4 oil pressure dropped way down. Figuring we had an oil leak, I feathered it and we turned back still loaded. We started to lose altitude but it didn't worry me because I thought we could hold 17,000 OK.

17,000 came and went. 16,500 came and went and we found ourselves in instrument conditions. I told the engineer to throw out the gas drums, unfeathered the engine, and with only 10 pounds of oil pressure ran it at 43 mikes to get back to 16,500. The main hatch release handle broke, and the men had to open the door instead of jettisoning it, and bad buffeting started. We all had chutes on and were ready to leave her. They finally got three drums out, but the fourth stuck in the door.

By this time, we had almost gotten to Shinbwiyang where 14,000 feet is safe and I feathered the engine again for fear of fire. The Number 3 supercharger regulator was also bad and the manifold pressure oscillated about three inches. Finally got into the valley and at low altitude got the other drum unstuck and part of the door closed. Hope the drum didn't land on the Barrys' house.

Came in for a landing but Lofland wouldn't do as I said, so we did the worst thing possible – overshot and had to go around. The next time we got in, me sighing with relief that Number 3 hadn't quit too.

May 31 – Got paid and beaten at chess. Put together a volleyball team for a tournament. I was scheduled for O.D. but it was called off when I got called over to Headquarters and ordered to go to Sookerating on temporary duty to act as defense counsel in a general court martial. Why me I don't know never having even seen a GCM, but I guess the defendant and me are stuck. Received orders putting me officially on the list as a Check Pilot over the Hump and on Instrument Board.

Jun. 1 – Took shuttle to Sookerating. Met the Trial Judge Advocate, Lt. Peickert, called in from Chabua. The defendant, Lt. Ford, is up on violation of 3 A.W. Lt. Ruggeri from Chabua is supposed to assist me. Ford, however, had a special defense counsel in mind from Ledo, so we went up there to see him. He's a Miami Beach lawyer and fairly sharp, having gotten several men off from charges and then being made TJA for the whole Ledo area.

The Ledo road is something terrific – a constant fog of dust from the swarm of trucks on it, the 20th and 48th General Hospitals being at Ledo, as well as all the depots for the road. It's like a World War I movie.

I talked to the lawyer, Lt. Frank, who doesn't seem to worry about the case, and then went over to see a couple of nurses Ford knew. They gave me ice cream and ice tea and a touch of American women talk, which sounded good. Got back to Sookerating at 04:00.

Jun. 2 – Lt. Frank came down from Ledo and we drew up a defense, interviewed witnesses and talked it over with Ford. Took all day long.

Up there the pilots are split into four areas, each centered around a former manager's "bungalow," and it would be good if they had enough bearers and transportation. They don't, so it isn't.

Went to the show and ran into Charlie Thieriot, who is flying 46s over the Hump. He's just arrived and is a snake pilot. He has about 2,400 hours in the air, mostly as a civilian instructor. He looks the same as he did at school, except much balder.

Jun. 3 – Talked the Major up there out of the L-5 and flew down to Tezpur with Bill Smith from Sookerating. I'll stay here until Wednesday and then go back for the trial. Being only an assistant there's not much for me to do, and Heaven knows what my assistant, whom I never saw, will do.

No mail since I left.

Col. Baber, Black Bob Baber, has been named Deputy Head of the Wing, and we are now in for drill, classes and calisthenics every day. The old, old story!

Six guys from here went home, including Murray and Hamilton, and according to McCallum I'm in for my promotion. Finally! I hope ...

Jun. 4 – Read, wrote Nance and Janie, and caught up on my log book. Played chess and dice, then got called up for a flight at 22:00.

Jun. 5 – Off the ground at 01:25. There was some instrument work, but weather was generally pretty good. Went to Chengtu by north course by nothing but D.R. (Dead Reckoning). The homing beacons at Lijiang, Sichang and Chengtu were out, and we had to come in to the latter by homing in on the tower. Royal and Young were in #588, the ship I lost an engine in, and were in bad trouble. Completely lost for three hours, north and east of Kunming, and a supercharger went out. They radioed they were going to bail out but the ground station talked them into Kunming, finally.

Haynie and McClean, in #606, are lost. Apparently they were lost and they lost an engine. They called for a bearing and got one from Chengtu indicating they were on course from Ipin to Chengtu. Haynie acknowledged bearing and then radioed that they were losing altitude and were ready to bail out. There was no further contact, but the man in the tower at Chengtu, two men on the ground, and Robbins and Jackson flying back all saw a big flare up and explosion about 15 minutes later, from the direction he was supposed to be. We looked for an hour but couldn't find the plane or the crew.

Then a Jorhat ship radioed that they were bailing out west of Yunnanyi, but they managed to make it back to Yunnanyi even with only three engines at 11,000 feet. Then there was a red alert at Chabua. Plenty of action. People here thought we were down too, as they had had no word of us until we started back.

Haynie and McClean today, a Jorhat ship yesterday, Misamari's Chief Pilot the day before, two more almost gone today and me almost gone 4 days ago! This business of Hardin's 24 hours a day schedule regardless of weather is bringing what we all expected!

Classes in ground school have started.

Skip-bombed the Barry's with a can of pate de foie gras and almost took the top off their gum tree with me. Pretty tired after nine and a half hours of flying and no sleep.

Jun. 6 – Relaxed for coming trial. Drank with Miller and Agnew and then tried to play poker. Now have 20 rupees to last me all month.

Jun. 7 – Flew to Sookerating and talked over the case with Frank and Ford. It looks pretty good.

Jun. 8 – Trial started at 09:00 and finished at 20:00. Frank did his best, but Ford faced a hostile court and he was convicted, with a dismissal from service recommended. It was a ridiculous decision but they were making an example of him. I believe it will be reversed on review.

Bill Cochran, a Major and Executive Officer at Chabua was on the court. Apparently Chick Reider is at a field near there too.

Jun. 9 – Flew down in L-5 with Bill Smith and renewed my skip-bombing practice on the Barrys with a carton of cigarettes and hit the lawn right in front of them!

Jun. 10 – Checked Brise today and we had a swell flight together to Kunming and back. We had to hold over Kunming for two hours, and hold every thousand feet down from 20,000 on instruments, but it was smooth and we broke out with an 800-foot ceiling. Not bad in the monsoons.

Dropped a note on the Barrys on the way back. Brise is now a Class-2 C-87 pilot. It sure is a pleasure to fly with someone who can fly as well as be enjoyable company.

Jun. 11 – Hit the jackpot on mail. Four wonderful letters from Nance full of details on the new apartment which sounds swell and very convenient. News of Jack Hulsne's death in the crash of a blimp, Betty's mumps which Nance passed, and pictures of Peter and Mike. I would never have recognized Mike, who was just an amiable lump when I left. Gosh how I wish I was home. Also a letter from Dad, Marmie and Townie Winmill.

Got called for a flight about 18:00 to fly as check pilot with Schnitzer, the Montclair boy. All went well till we were near Tali, then the controls tightened up. No ice. Next the plane did its best to turn over four times. Schnitz and I were both using full controls, throttle wide open and stick full-forward. 60 degrees from one side to the other it lurched, and then slowly straightened out. We had lost 2,800 feet and only had 14,800 left. Tali is at 15,200. Luckily we were slightly south of it. In all my flying I've never had anything remotely resembling it or quite as dangerous, as the maneuvers were so violent there wasn't a chance of getting out of the ship.

After it was over the controls felt like mildewed bananas, and we did not know whether to bail out, dump the load and land, or stay with it. One word from me, and all I needed was for one engine to sputter, and we would have all jumped. But we tested it out in 30 degree banks, and at 145 with half flaps, and decided to land, which we did at 150 MPH!

Checked all controls on the ground and could find nothing wrong. We had had no ice, no rough air, and controls don't tighten up before a stall, and planes don't stall at 155 indicated – and yet we were as close to crashing as I've ever been.

Jun. 12 – Flew back, and the plane was still sloppy every time we hit the slightest rough air. I've now lost an engine and had one catch on fire on takeoff. I've lost one engine empty over Tali. I've lost one loaded over the Hump and been going down on instruments at night on the Hump. I've overshot the runway on three engines at night. I've been chased off a runway by bombing raids. I've flown 700 miles by dead reckoning. I've been lost at night in thunderstorms. I've had a plane do its best to try flying on its back at night. I've flown through more thunderstorms than I knew existed, and been weighted down with ice with a snow storm in the cockpit. St. Elmo's Fire has been all over the plane. I've let down between thunderstorms from 20,000 feet – and yet I've never quite had to bail out.

So when I got back this morning I cornered Maj. Gownes, the C.O., and Maj. Cowan, the Operations Officer, and asked about a promotion. They think it's in but they don't really know! That's the payoff. They better get it here quick or I'll be spending the next six months walking out of the Hump if I'm lucky!

Jun. 13 – Recovered from yesterday. Read and wrote.

Jun. 14 – Haynie and McClean are OK. They're in the hospital at Chengtu. Haynie has a broken ankle and McClean a lacerated tongue. It should be the other way around.
Ted Griggs, a St. Paul MN boy and a Yale classmate, showed up as a captain and navigator of a B-29 last night and today. Apparently the B-29s are having engine trouble and they are losing a lot. They've been on a couple of raids in the South Pacific

and lost six, though they've yet to see a Jap. I understand that tomorrow they are gathering at Chengtu for a raid on Tokyo! They'll probably lose a lot as it's a long way, but the kids are itching to go.

Flew to Chengtu with Collins and counted 18 B-29s. It seems they are assembling for tomorrow. Had a good trip except for the inevitable thunderstorms in the valley – came through three of them.

Lofland reported lost. No word from him since last night. He was flying Number 556, old Pork Chop, which could almost get there on its own reputation.

Jun. 15 – I was approached by Capt. Scott to help him out in his court martial arising out of shooting a G.I. in his basha. Don't really want to, but I guess I will if one isn't appointed.

Night flight to Chanyi with a Jorhat pilot. He did a good job but made his approach too low to suit me. We had a cargo of extra-sensitive bombs and 100-octane gas on board. What a beautiful rocket we might have made!

About 30 Jorhat pilots and half their ships have been transferred here while Jorhat takes on a special assignment with C-46s.

The Tokyo raid came off, but I don't have any details on it yet.

Jun. 16 – Got back from the trip at 09:00 and slept till 16:00. I got a note from Abie Barry asking me out on the 18th and telling me that my skip-bombing with the pate de foie gras had been very accurate. Apparently I came within ten feet of scoring a direct hit on Marion! Finished a letter to the family.

Jun. 17 – Got called for an early flight to Chengtu with Captain Galbraith. He had been in the RAF and had been on 26 missions, has flown in Alaska as a bush pilot, and he looks like somebody's Aunt Maude.

We started off but had to turn back on account of a leaking cargo drum, and the second time Number 1 tachometer went out at 2300 RPMs and wouldn't budge. Third time out, an electrical fire started behind the instrument panel. On the fourth try, I ordered everyone to don the chutes, but we got it out and made it back OK.

I'll try to get to the Barrys for a day. No word on Lofland, and I guess he is definitely lost. No word at all so he probably blew up or turned over and hit a mountain.

Thank Heaven the invasion is progressing! The Jap one on Hunan and Chengtu is also progressing, damn it!

Went to Pertalguhr with Fletcher and Mr. McWilliams, another tea planter. He is a bachelor who spends more time entertaining American flying officers than he does on tea, and in many ways he reminds me of one of P.G. Wodehouse's characters, Freddy Featherstone, as he would be in middle age. Amusing and likable, but definitely simple-minded.
The Barrys greeted us with open arms and offers of "battes." Apparently my accuracy in skip-bombing is terrific. The pate landed ten feet from Marion on the front lawn, the cigarettes just one side of the lawn, and the matches with the note on the upper tennis court, which is really part of the front lawn. I gather they could do with a little less accuracy and more safety.

Jun. 18 - Rained all day, so after the usual wonderful meals and sleep we played golf instead of tennis. We quit after the ninth hole as there was a party at the club to see the movie Fletcher had arranged, "The More the Merrier." There were the usual G.I. shorts boasting of America before, and as usual I got very embarrassed. It's funny how much of a booster country we are until you show some movies like that to someone not American. I cringed, but they were very polite and clapped heartily. I've been invited to come whenever I could, and Abie invited Harvey and me to go to Shillong with him in August. I believe it's off-limits but Marian said she'd find out and write us. Going to a place like that with someone to help us get started should be real fun.

Jun. 19 - Left early - back at base I heard that another ship had crashed, this time in the pattern at Chengtu and killed all hands. That's the third time in three weeks or less.

Jun. 20 - Was scheduled for a flight when I got a call from Lt. Peickert, the opposing Trial Judge Advocate in the case at Sookerating. I had been ordered to defend a general court martial case against a boy at Misamari. Flew over in the PT-17 with Emerson Sturdevant, my assistant. The court wanted to try the case tomorrow morning and I only got there at 2:30 PM. Told them we couldn't possibly be ready for at least a day, then started investigating and found our client to be guilty as hell; he actually wanted a dismissal from the service.

As a matter of prestige, we persuaded him to plead "Not Guilty" after an hour argument with him. That's perfectly legal as it merely requires the prosecution to prove their case and is expressly provided for in the manual. Then we looked for character witnesses, but not a man would testify for him. We discovered that the chief prosecution witness was slightly deaf and might not be sure of what our client had told him to do ("burn uncensored and unposted enlisted men's mail to get rid of it.") I drew up a couple of motions and we interviewed people all day.

Jun. 21 - Interviews and studying law - about 6:30 after going to bed at 2:30 and we didn't stop work till 1 am. Both of us hated the guy and had no sympathy for the things he'd done, but we were supposed to defend him and we sure did our best.

Jun. 22 - We won our motion to strike one specific action and we left them the hardest to prove. We pinned our hopes on the deafness charge but we had no witnesses except the medical one, and we couldn't put the defendant on the stand. It took the court 40 minutes to decide after the case was closed, so at least we won the moral victory. If we got him off after the Sookerating case, I would've really felt badly.

Word has apparently gone out for the courts to give the defendants all they can give if they find them guilty: one poor guy who beat up another officer not only got dismissed but got five years at hard labor besides. He's only just 20, and was urged on to beat this guy up by two captains, neither of whom was charged, though one will probably be thrown out by reclassification proceedings.

Jun. 23 - Got back here to find everyone going crazy over here - Goodman and Tutt, both captains, fighting in the club, Captain Slip hitting another guy with a chromium chair and a big ruckus in town in which Sandy Agnew was involved.

Jun. 24 - Not hungry so I didn't eat all day. Hotter than hell! Club council meeting with Maj. Keffer - ban Goodman, Tutt and Slip from the club for a month, thank Heaven. Maybe we can calm the guys down before they all get court-martialed. Was called for a flight at 10 pm. Took off at 11:55 pm.

Jun. 25 - Our anniversary (of the day we announced our engagement four years ago!) And what a wonderful four years ...

Flew to Chungking in the B-24 tanker, giving R.O. Smith a Class 1 check. He did a pretty good job. Coming back, we flew through a thunderstorm and actually got hit by lightning. No damage done but it scared the pants off us. He really had to sweat when I cut an engine on the landing, but got it in without any help needed.

Jun. 26 - Loafed and read all day.

Jun. 27 - Actually got up for breakfast! Wrote a story to Peter, and wrote Aunt Helen. Ran into Eddie Dwyer, a roommate at Turner and a swell guy. He's stationed at Agra flying copilot on a 47 after instructing in them at St. Joe! He's going to try and bring some milk up here. Got the orders out banning Slip, Goodman and Tutt from the club for a month.

Got a package from Martin's Fruit Shop addressed to Sgt. Peter Dominick from Margaret Barbero in Newburgh, New York. Couldn't understand it as I've never heard of her and I thought maybe it was a gift from some Italian club; but after opening it and admiring her choice, I found it was supposed to be for Lt. Barbero here, and I had to give it up. He'll probably get one for me one of these days.

Called for a flight in the middle of a volleyball game and got a 1st pilot trip. Trip okay, but the ship was no good: couldn't hold 17,500 at 150 mph with 34° manifold pressure and 2200 RPM and 5° of flaps. If we'd ever lost an engine we were all through, so I turned it in as unsafe to fly.

Jun. 28 - Went to bed for remainder of day.

Jun. 29 - Trip to Chengtu with Retz. Daytime trip and weather fair for this time of year. Heard that Kweilin is being evacuated and gas dropped on all the boys! This Jap drive is pretty serious. Boys all ready to leave Chengtu, if they head west instead of continuing south. The Japs claim they'll do both and have Chengtu by the end of the summer. I don't see why not. There's nothing to stop them except for a few low mountains and then the '29s will have to move way back.

Jun. 30 - Tried to sleep some. Wrote brief letters to Nance – got equally brief one from her. Was called for a flight about 6 PM.

The Diary
Part 4

Jul. 1 - Finally got back. Had bad icing conditions to Chengtu, and then Snyder, a service pilot captain, got screwed up and had to make three passes to get in field. He wouldn't go around soon enough and twice we almost smashed into hills at the end of the runway. Then the ship broke a supercharger and we waited and took back another they'd just finished fixing.

Jul. 2 - Trip to Chengtu checking out a Maj. Johnston. He's a really good pilot but the ice situation was awful. We had a good 1.5 inches of clear rinse ice all over the ship, didn't dare go lower than 18,000 feet and couldn't get over it even at 24,000. Slugged home with high power settings and flaps and prayed we wouldn't get lost. Radio useless because of ice, and piton heads almost fell off plane.

Jul. 3 - Eureka! A free day – only I was made Trial Judge Advocate in a special court martial case and was told to get it going as soon as possible. Maybe I'll win a case. Letter from Nance dated June 15th.

Jul. 4 - Trip to Chungking. Weather was pretty good, but the pilot, Capt. J. R. Martin, was unsure of himself and almost ran out of runway. Had to partially ground loop plane to stop only 15 feet from edge of strip with a ditch at the end. Two ships were shot down today just north of Myitkyina. Crews got out but we don't know whether they landed in Japanese or American territory. From Myitkyina to Paoshan is all Jap territory. Not a firecracker!

Jul. 5 - Served papers on a defendant who is up for a special court martial on two innocuous charges after Wing refused to charge manslaughter, though he had shot and killed a native in a local brawl. Interviewed witnesses and talked to Sandy Agnew, who is in serious trouble over an affair in town.

Jul. 6 – Spent all day in town trying to influence the Duchi's, a family half-Italian and half-Indian, not to press charges. They had already done so to the post, the town police and the Indian government. Got them to agree to drop all charges, and then found that didn't clear the military angle here, as the investigation had already begun. Again I risked life and limb and talked them into changing their testimony so that it now appears that Sandy was acting in self-defense. Got through about midnight.

Jul. 7 – Prosecuted case and the boy got four months in the clink at hard labor. Too much for the things he was charged with and not enough for what he should have been charged with if Wing is going to be consistent.

Featherstone popped up. He's at Sylhet in a special group flying 47's to supply our troops around Imphal. Apparently the group is the result of a hurry call from Lord Mountbatten to General Arnold.

Letter from Nance dated 17th of June! Mail is sure getting slow!

Jul. 8 – Finished record this afternoon and got Agnew's statement in to Sturdevant, the investigating officer. I may get him out with nothing at all, or the 104, or it may go to a General Court. If it does, we now have a chance! Heard through Intelligence that the Japs had gassed Kweilin again and shot the pilot of one of the 46 crews after he gave the Burmese all his rupees to take him back to Americana troops. A great bunch of people – damn their miserable hides! Thank Heaven the B-29's hit Japan proper again.

Nance's picture completed and it's damn good. Wrote Nance and Sly Corbett, and family and Nance yesterday. Still no word on how Hi Randel is coming along. Mr. Babb in Bombay has my camera and is sending it along.

Jul. 9 – Stackman and Holton have disappeared in plane. No word at all but we hope it's at Chengtu. Holton lives next door where Harwell lived. The crew chief of the C-46 was also shot by the Japs and they broadcast it! Wrote Mr. Babb for camera.

A Misamari ship blew up on takeoff. Griffin cracked up ship at Chanyi. Hall and Stafford were fired at over Myitkyina by Jap ackack. I started off giving Galbraith a Class 1 check and we had a leaky gas drum in the nose. The fumes were so bad in the air that our eyes smarted and watered and we didn't dare even use our radio. One spark would've blown us higher than the Misamari job, which we saw light up the sky 25 miles away. Returned and it was too late to take off by the time it was fixed, as we couldn't have gotten a night landing in China.

Jul. 11 – Stackman and Heller still missing. This business of merely disappearing is getting us down. No radio word of anything wrong. They just take off and disappear with no word at all.

Wonderful letter from Nance which cheered me up a little. Heller was a good friend of mine, a check pilot and a good one too. Carriotti lived just two bashas down and was on our volleyball team. Went on check with Galbraith. Trip OK except for a lost horizon instrument.

Jul. 12 – Stackman turned up. Crashed near Tsuyung south of Yunnanyi. He and the engineer are in the hospital. Holton is dead, and the radio operator, apparently the only one to bail out, is still missing.

Slept most of the day. Today is our forth wedding anniversary and the third when we've been apart. We sure run into tough luck on them.

Jul. 13 – Was called about 10 am for a Class 2 check. Good trip going over but coming back we just bored into one thunderstorm after another. The lightning was so bad and so brilliant that we had to turn on all the cockpit lights so we wouldn't be blinded by it. St. Elmo's fire made a fiery cross out of us all the way.

Charlie Heller's ship has been found. The only survivor apparently is Carriotti. They crashed just north of Myitkyina near Warazup. No word on the reason for either ship going down; at least they've been found, which is more than Lofland ever was.

We now have no chairs in our basha. Air Corps Supply took them all. Johnson moved next door, where Holton and Harwell were, which seems very unwise to me, so Staf. and I are again sole inmates of this crazy house.

Jul. 14-15 – Had a 1st Pilot trip at last. Good trip to Chengtu and back with Lt. Freeman. News on Stackman and Heller: apparently Stackman's ship developed a very bad tail flutter and then he claims the rudder became inoperative. He ordered the men to bail out and for some reason they didn't do it. So he bailed out first to lead the way. He didn't tell them where they were or which direction to walk. The engineer followed him and presumably the radio operator. Holton, the co-pilot, had buckled the leg straps of his chute over his safety belt and was frantically struggling to get up when they left. He didn't get out.

The engineer started walking southeast, the general route to Kunming, but from where he was it would have landed him in the Jap lines. Luckily he stopped to rest, and Stackman had sent out guides who found him and brought him back. Still no word on the radio operator.

Heller's ship flew into a thundercloud which was so rough it spilled their gyro instruments. They tried to fly it on needle and ball but they were already in a spiral and couldn't get it out. Heller yelled to bail out and Carriotti got up to do so. He lost consciousness before bailing out and came to falling through the air. He pulled his ripcord and landed OK. Apparently the ship, which was in a tight spiral and had an indicated airspeed of 300 mph, had hit a pocket of air and torn the wing off the plane. The center section of the wing is over the flight deck, and apparently Carriotti was sucked out. He didn't have his chute buckled up and was hanging by one arm when he came to. No word on any of the other crew members.

Went into town and bought some chairs to use in the basha. Had dinner at the Chinese restaurant. Told Dunaway I would not go to Gaya for instructor school.

Jul. 16 – Rumor has it that a big A.T.C. group is going to be started in Australia to supply the Islands. Colonel Estelle will be there. Maybe I can transfer when I'm through here. Was called to the line to talk over the Gaya deal; I finally agreed to go when

I was told they had iced drinks, Coca Cola, ice cream and good food, and when they agreed that I could stop instructing after 14 more trips.

Jul. 17 – Won 100 rupees in a crap game! No mail for the last week. Read and played chess.

Jul. 18 - Got orders, and through Lex Durham, now a captain, got a ride on the ASC shuttle plane to Labrurnishat. From there to Gaya. Am in with a C-47 driver from Lalhat and a C-46 pilot from Mohanbari. Schwartz and Mischler, respectively. Galbraith down here as an instructor. And I just finished checking him! Anyhow we sat in the bar and chewed the fat and I got a lot of news out of him. Col. Baker has been put in charge of the valley, which is to be known as the ABC wing. Col. Baker, besides being a heel in my opinion, is a service pilot and a Wilmington Ferry Group man. Result: service pilots are flooding in and taking over all the new jobs, and they all come from Wilmington.

Tezpur gets a new C.O., a Major Farkwell, very soon, and probably a new Operations officer, Capt. Galbraith. Hayne will come back as chief pilot for a short time, and then be replaced by someone from Wilmington. Gen. Hardin will have charge of the western sector, and Gen. Turner of the east. Both Baker and Turner are strict disciplinarians, and I foresee hours of ground school and calisthenics.

Jul. 19-24 – School – Ground school! Passed four out of five subjects, so I only have to take radio courses and stuff like "How To Instruct in 3 Easy Lessons." Had four hours flying with Galbraith and their ship out for engine change. Had two hours link work. Haven't learned a thing, don't like their school or their procedures for flying, won't use them, extreme inefficiency on setup, but I have fair food and cold drinks and occasionally ice cream. I'll stay till end of week, and if the ship's not in I plan to just leave anyhow! Made some good friends, notably Don Mischler and Bob Schwartz.

Jul. 25-30 – Still here and ship still not. Tried to leave but the Colonel wouldn't let me. Had three hours in a C-46 and three in a C-47. Had another link period, and the rest of the time I sat around doing nothing. Retook weather exam to get a higher mark.

Conference of school: I sounded off and told them it wasn't any use. Created quite a stir. The Colonel went to Gen. Hardin, and heads will fall all over the valley until they do what Wing says right or wrong. I believe the colonel is on our side. Galbraith is to be Wing Chief Pilot. He wants me to stay here and instruct in his place, but I refused. He added I might be Chief Pilot of Tezpur after Guyton, who took McCallum's place who went home. Spent all afternoon telling everyone that school was useless in its present state, would be useless anyhow, and even if it wasn't they couldn't run it without equipment. Between me and Fischer, who purposely did very badly and when called in to explain told them all what he thought of a) the school, b) service pilots in general, and c) their methods and procedures, I don't believe we're popular.

Went swimming yesterday in Gaya; Hoke and Hall down here from Tezpur to be the next suckers. What a mess! Bought two pairs of boots for myself to celebrate my 29th year and my 24th going to school!

Jul. 31-Aug. 3 – Flew 5:30 in C-46 and D-24 my last day and on August 1, after taking a written exam in both 46 and 47 was given proficiency slips in both.

Bought two nice purses for Nance and Marmie, and a pair of boots for Peter. Had 10 rupees when I left. Flew up to Chabua with the colonel, Galbraith, Mischler and McCorkle and spent night. Got shuttle to Tezpur yesterday, and am really glad to get back. Reported in and found Tweed is Assistant Chief Pilot. Both he and Guyton should be leaving soon.

My back's in bad shape where I fell into the catwalk of a B-24 the last day of Gaya, so I went to Doc's. Just bone bruises, but got put on DNIF. Got 5 packages and about 20 letters. Got a statue of Mike, bracelet, watch, cookies and candles, inflatable pillow, magnifying glass, sketching materials, etc.

We have a new Executive Officer, a service pilot, Major Pratt. Also two new Majors flying as line pilots, both service pilots. Was on orders, but taken off to defend a court martial case in Sookerating. Also missed a special court martial here.

Letter from Dave, Jr., Townie, who is here in theater but in western division, Bud Parks and Harlan, besides "Lou," Nance and family. Also Rannie and Mr. Babb. My camera is on its way.

Brise cracked up on takeoff at Chunking when nose door opened, but though cockpit and ship demolished, no one was hurt. Boy were they lucky.

Aug. 3-13 – Had four trips, three pretty good ones and one bad. Usual storms, etc., but hit hail squalls that dented leading edges of wings and lightning hit twice and knocked out radio. Had another fire at end of another trip. If anything gets me, it will be fire in the air, I'm sure.

My promotion has been turned down again. Apparently they are all frozen, though if the C.O. writes a special letter, you get one. Then I was called over to explain deficit in club funds. Was informed that as Assistant Chief Pilot I wouldn't get as much time or get home as soon. Bitched to C.O. on promotion and got nowhere. I told Pratt I didn't know anything about deficit

Flying the Hump

and cared less and I resigned. Also resigned from instructing. Meeting called of all officers on club deal and I was put back on committee, damn it. Also told I couldn't resign from instructing job and that my official records showed fifty hours less time than my own log so there's another loss.

Had an interesting talk at Gaya by a liaison officer between Americans and Chinese. Apparently Chinese shoot at anything at night, so no matter who you are, don't approach them at night. Face means a lot, so if they are ordered to take a certain position they always claim they have whether they actually have or not. The Americans at Myitkyina didn't realize this at first and would rely on the word that the Chinese had captured the position and thereby get outflanked. Furthermore, they (the Chinese) don't know any offensive maneuvers so they attack head on into a series of machine guns and die by the thousands. The Americans actually captured Myitkyina once when the Japs surrendered. As they came out under a white flag the Chinese shot them anyhow so the Japs naturally ducked back and dug in. One of Seagroves' doctors was there as well as one of Merrill's Marauders, so it was pretty interesting.

Zeros are out again. One of the boys attacked two days ago but got in clouds O.K. Staf. gone on leave. Got ibex wool coat for Nance.

Aug. 13-24 – Had four trips and three local periods, so have been pretty busy flying. And my luck seems to be changing as I've only had one bad time in the flying. They opened up new fields around Chengtu and I went into Kuangnan, one N.E. of Hsiching, at 2:00 am with absolutely no briefing except the tower frequency. We did not know where the hills were, how long the runway was, how many obstructions there were, the lights on the runway were only candlepower, and the thick haze made our landing lights bounce off and do no good. Martin couldn't get lined up, and when I finally shoved the coal to her we only

Dad receives his Air Medal from General Hardin.

had 150 feet left and he was trying to make a 40° turn into runway. We found out the hard way that there were no obstructions as we floated along at 300 feet. Finally made an 800-foot pattern and 30-second base leg to get in.

Gen. Hardin arrived and pinned some medals on some of us. Stuck me with the Air Medal. Checked up to find I'm in, and have been since July 8th, for the D.F.C. Might get it in December. We then had "General Hardin Day," the biggest mass bottom-kissing in history.

On a designated day everyone held up their planes and then started sending them over at 7:00 pm to see whether they could break the tonnage record, and I imagine we succeeded as we put out one-third again as many trips as ever before and we were all going to fields just the other side of the Hump instead of Chengtu so we could carry more cargo. I went to Yunnanyi in the daytime too. Marvelous trip for a change. The usual Jap Zeros were sighted 15 minutes south of Yunnanyi just as I took

off but I'm so blind I probably wouldn't have seen them if they'd been up my tail.

Finally got sick. Thought it was malaria but discovered it was only faintness from not having eaten in two weeks so I went to the Chinese restaurant and had some good food.

No promotions this month, only one next month and one the month after. Was informed I had too much Hump time to go in as Assistant Chief pilot as I would be going home too soon. Also had too much time to merely fly myself as I would like, and so I have to continue instructing. No captaincy now, I guess.

A feud is going on against our Operations Officer who runs this place like a czar and has managed to get himself 65 day trips to China in the best weather and an Air Medal and DFC on his own recommendation and a captaincy after only six months in grade. The boys got up and protested volubly.

Brise got rooked again: he only had 200 hours to go to finish and for no reason they suddenly transferred him to China to be an operations officer there. And no promotion to take the sting out. We went to see very high mogul, but they wouldn't release him.

Just heard Dick Dominick has been wounded. The first of the clan and I hope the only one. The Allies are in Paris and have landed in southern France and have taken Marseilles, the French patriots are taking over Southwest France, and today Rumania quit – the second jackal out of the pack! Eight more guys went home, and George Cricenti took the white ibex wool evening coat to Nance for me. Hope she likes it. Sent a purse to Nance and another one to Marmie. Bought a jade bracelet and ordered a carved, wooden-handled carving set. Will try to get the sapphire bracelet if I can scrape the dough together.

Aug. 24-Sept. 4 – The main item has been flying as I've put in over 50 hours in this time between the Hump and local work. The weather has gotten very bad again, apparently the tail end of the monsoon proving it still has a stinger. Informed I had too much time to be Chief or Assistant Chief Pilot. O.K. by me as I'll get home sooner. Then got definite word all promotions frozen till December anyhow, so I won't get my captaincy over here. It will take nine months after I get home, and that will make 29 months in grade. Not a bad record.

Had two ships lost: one went in on final at Chunking due to pilot error due to too much flying. The other, with Dunaway, just disappeared and we've had no word on it. There is a terrible shortage of pilots and radio operators, and the boys are getting too much flying, the average last month being 137 hours. I was below average with 123 hours, but 100 of that was night time and my hair is really getting grey.

The European setup sure seems wonderful. Maybe the war there will be over before I get home! Been teaching Houston chess ever since Brise left. Stafford back from leave and the basha is no longer a restful haven.

Got orders to go to Chabua as Assistant Defense Counsel in court martial case. Got out of it by telling executive officer here, Major Giberson since May (Pratt went to take charge of Misamari) how much work I was doing instructing - then went down and got out of instructing. I'm now a cross between a G.I. pilot and an air instructor but at least I'll get some left seat time.

Went to the monkey temple in town, a very old Hindu temple with the conical stone roofs stained by monkeys, pigeons and monsoon seasons. It's in a big grove of shade trees and literally hundreds of monkeys jump through the trees, sit on the roof picking ticks and fleas off each other and chattering at visitors. And the priest, a regular dirty Indian with carefully dressed hair on his head, upper lip and chin, comes up and says, "The grace of God be with you. And for that I expect something for myself." When accused of getting rich quick he replies with a frank grin and says, "Why not?" There were carvings of Gonesh and Siwa on the front portals and he told me some of the legends built on them. All pretty fascinating, gynecological and fantasies (sic).

Should be through and ready to go home in a month. Boy, will that be marvelous. I only have 120 hours to go. Wonder what to do about my grey hair!

The Diary
Part 5

Sept. 5-13 – My camera finally arrived and I've been busy taking pictures of everything Indian and Chinese. I've got so much film I'll never use it all up, damn it.

Still flying a lot, and it's still as varied as ever. Old 590, my ship, stalled out at 150 right over the Hump and we lost 1,500 feet before she would recover. We kept going, and coming back two different parts caught fire. The next trip was a real dilly. I had a new copilot and we went out to the plane, full of vim and vigor – and the radio was out. Two hours later that was fixed, and then the anti-icer didn't work on number 3 and 4 engines. This caused another delay. When we were finally ready we only had seven minutes before our waiting period of five hours would be up.

We took off and everything went well till we got about 40 minutes past the first ridge. Suddenly the number one engine manifold pressure and tachometer started dancing around and the engine ran away. I reached up, hit the feather button and started to turn around. The engine wouldn't feather, so we cut off the mixture, turbo, booster pump, throttle, ignition and gas pump and kept it at 2500 RPM. Number two engine started in to do the same thing and I feathered that. By this time, we were down to 15,800 feet and still losing altitude. Sent the crew chief back to dump the load and got the radioman to send out a distress signal. Then, as it was obvious we would have to bail out with only two engines left, we unfeathered number two engine and managed to get it running. It stayed OK from then on, thank Heaven, until near the end.

At this point, the crew chief came up and told me that the violent lurch I had just noticed was caused by having the door go through the tail surface while falling off. We had full trim and both of us on the rudder to hold it even. We were losing altitude rapidly and it looked as if we weren't going to get back over the first ridge of the valley. I gave the word to prepare to bail out. We notified all stations of our position.

Then I thought of a fighter strip fairly close to us and I headed for that. Number one prop was flat side to the breeze and caught fire. Pulled fire extinguisher. We were down to 8,000 feet and still losing altitude with 47" of M.P. on the other three engines. We were getting to the fighter strip but still couldn't see it when they turned their homing off! Managed to get it turned on again by radio calls. Found field nestled in a cup of hills going up to 10,000 feet. We had 5,000 and were holding finally. Edged into cup through river pass. Started making right-hand pattern and lost field. Started over and made left pattern. Number one on fire again. Got on downwind and found we couldn't get far enough away from field to make a pattern! Lost all flight instruments and number two engine. Edged into hills over trees, took one last look, cut power and made a 45° banking 180° approach, dropping flaps and gear at the same time. Luckily they came down. Aimed short of runway and plowed through sand on final. Approach was just right, but when I started flare out the four drums in the nose wouldn't come up. Stood up and yanked on elevators. It eased over a ditch and lit on end, and we stopped two-thirds up a 4,000-foot runway!

Hopped out after cutting switches for fear of an explosion, but fire died out. The strip was in Shinbwiyang in Burma, site of an A.S.C. and fighter outfit, and we were the first four-engine job to get in there. The jungle around there is really thick. It took one reserve squadron five days to go five miles in to get a guy who crashed and the leeches almost finished them. The Ledo road runs through there and we were paralleling it just in case we had to bail out, but even so they told us we would have been lucky to find it even if we landed only 100 yards away from it.

Took some pictures and shot the bull with Major Bray, the C.O. of the A.S.C. unit. The tents they sleep in are covered with mold from the jungle dampness, and the bugs are bad, but the morale is pretty good. The difference between the A.S.C. and a combat unit. Major Cowan came in on a 47 the next day and told me with a grin that since we brought it in we could get it out, and added that we were pretty lucky. Which we were: usually the field is socked in. I was amused by the complete absence of a pat on the back!

The next trip we lost a turbo and came back empty on three engines. The next was with my new roommate, a sleepy Texas boy by the name of Roy Clark, who knew nothing about the Hump or the plane, and I had to do all the flying, all the procedures and most of the radio work. Succeeded in making the worst landing of my career at Chengtu, but nothing broke.

The Japs now have night fighters over the Hump, and we have to fly with no navigation, cockpit or running lights on, which makes it rough as there are so many planes in the air. Japs are in the outskirts of Kweilin, which is being evacuated, and they have been bombing the Chengtu area as well as shooting up planes and auxiliary fields with night fighters and fighter bombers.

13 more guys on orders to go home today. I should be on about next month, or at least through by then as I only have 80 hours to go. I believe I'm the oldest inhabitant here now, and certainly the ranking first lieutenant. Damn it.

Sept. 14-22 – The C.O. woke me in the middle of the night of the 13th and asked whether I would accept a West trip! Imagine after pleading for one for eight months they wanted to know whether I would accept one. Flew to Barachpore outside of Calcutta and on to Bangalore on the 14th. Nice eight-hour daylight trip with Vincent, another first pilot and instructor.

Bangalore is in the southwest corner of India between Bombay and Ceylon, and is one of the better spots of India: cool, nice post, easy work, only reasonably dirty city, lots of British! Slept like a log under blankets. Left our bags on operation porch on advice of Lieutenant Sugarman, whom I knew through law practice, and went to town. Bought a scarf to match the coat I'd sent to Nance, some silk underwear and a little Indian bell. Passed up a topaz the size of a hen's egg as I already had the sapphire bought from Mrs. Friggers in Tezpur. When we got back from town we discovered some bright bearer had put both our bags on a plane to Ceylon, mine with my lens in it! Sent wires, but still haven't gotten them back! Plane still missing badly on number two engine, so we spent the night. Met Tweed on his way home covered with ribbons. He's taking a boat home by way of Bombay.

Flew back same way and landed at night. Told by Clark that the C.O. had been looking for me with orders to clear the post as I was transferred to Gaya as a Wing Instructor. Couldn't believe it. Only 50 hours to go, a little less than two weeks, and they transfer me! Saw Gownes and Cowan the next day and asked them what the deal was. Apparently my name came through on orders from Headquarters. Cowan said he had protested to the Colonel down at Gaya, to no avail. Both Gownes and Cowan refused to say I was necessary to the field and wouldn't go to bat for me as the orders were from Gen. Turner. I told them just what I thought of the deal and of them. Gownes grinned and said, "That's tough, son." Baloney.

Morale on the post went down even more when the guys found out what had happened to me. Cleared post and came down on the 19th. Found Charlie Thieriot and Don Mischler shanghaied down here on the same deal. Went to see Col. Willy. Argued solidly for a half-hour about how I was almost through, didn't like instructing, eyesight getting bad and didn't think I could handle it. At the end he said, "All you've said, Lieutenant, convinces me we want you. I don't want guys who think they're hot stuff!" Then I attacked him on the promotion deal. No soap.

Apparently you can't be recommended within three months of going home, though Mohanbari got 26 captains last month! Only field to get any! He promised to send my name in as soon as I was ready. According to the way they count time, 650 necessary in Hump work, 900 down here, but Hump time counting for time and a half. I only have eight hours to go. Beaver promised to send me in too, but I don't guess I'll get out for at least three more months. Word has it that the valley has been raised from 900 to 1,000 hours, which leaves me about 110 hours. Apparently the colonel remembered that I had been the one to suggest making this the standard transition school for India and not an instruction school and had looked up my record and sent for me. WHEN will I learn to keep my big yap closed?

Had three hours down here in three days, and things are almost as confused as ever. Food's worse, schedule is rough. Ships are mostly out of commission. Houston, Rice and Stafford are here as students. Houston brought the pooch, and apparently one night when she was tied outside, a bird attacked her, picked her up and started off. When the rope tightened she was dropped, hit a nerve and is completely paralyzed. Has been for three days.

But she's Chinese and tough, and she is eating and living and may pull through. Japs got Charlie Glass and his crew just before I left. That's four in the last month we've lost from Tezpur. Night fighters very active. The Jap push on Paoshan, Yunnanyi, and Kweilin going along fine for them, and the Hump is more dangerous that way than ever. And here I'm stuck!

Sept. 22-Oct. 9 – I've almost despaired of anything good coming out of this transfer. I've been here for some three weeks and have had to fight hard to get forty hours of flying in. We officially need 1,000 hours before going home, and even when you get it, your orders come through only in priority with how long you've been in India. I have some 85 hours to fly or at least 6 weeks before my name goes in. So Christmas at home is one more dream shot to hell by the Army. I asked the major whether I'd get a promotion. "Very improbable," he said, then added, "If you got it, would you accept a four-month extension of duty here?"

That's the final blow. I just don't give a damn any more. Apparently doing a good job means nothing. You get nothing out of it, not even an occasional helping hand. At Tezpur, Greenwood has gone home along with others who came when I did and had less time when they left than I do! Lost another ship: George Hunt, a young kid from Maine, half-Indian, was lost with his whole crew coming back from China. Believe he cracked up while letting down on instruments and running out of gas. Knew him pretty well as I checked him out! Promotions are now going through there as I knew they would as soon as I left. As the saying goes, "Things are tough all over."

We now have nine C-87 instructors and only three ships, all wrecks. Three others, worse wrecks, have all been grounded. I devised a new schedule but it wasn't accepted. Another one was put in whereby we only fly five out of 15 possible ships every period so engineering can get the rest working. Already we're behind, as only three ships, two C-46's and one C-87, are fit to fly!

Furthermore, with the amount of time we give these students it's criminal to send them out as first pilots over the Hump. I've written Bob Relze, Chief Pilot at Tezpur, and told him so, so they should get a pretty thorough check back there before being released. I fully expect the school to fold up in another two months. Just as a possible promotion should arrive here!

Between classes I went up to Patna with Galloway and Calloway, lieutenants, and four captains. The captains not only outranked us, they outnumbered us, which was important as we disagreed violently. We had guns with us on the chance we'd see some game, and they proceeded to polish off a bottle of rum and some beers, and then stop the car and take potshots at two innocent vultures. They didn't hit the buzzards, some 40 feet away, but how in the hell they missed the natives behind the buzzards I don't know. None of them knew how to handle a gun, and they brandished them around like short daggers, menacing everyone. The lieutenants banded together and took one guy's gun away, but could do nothing about the driving. We never went under 50, and his method of getting through the crowded Indian villages, where bullock carts, women with loads balanced on their heads, children, goats, pigs, dogs, chickens and cows wander around indiscriminately, was to hold his hand on the horn and his foot on the accelerator. We scraped a bridge and a bullock cart, but no damage was done, luckily.

Patna is an overgrown Indian village with a British end to it, but no Britishers were there and it rained continually. We went to the officers' club to promote some excitement and got so excited we returned and went to bed at 9 p.m. The hotel was dirty, the beds hard and the prices high. The next day the lieutenants drove so we could see some of the things we'd driven by so fast. The countryside is really beautiful: the green rice paddies, beautiful big trees, tall pahus and occasional abrupt hills to break the monotony of the flatness. But because of the Indians it's filthy dirty. It seems a shame to waste it so.

We passed a monkey deserted and alone in the middle of the big trees, and the trees and grass swarmed with healthy-looking monkeys: young ones getting free rides on their Ma, jumping from tree to tree and scolding like mad when I tried to get pictures. We also saw an Indian funeral, four men carrying a body on a rude stretcher covered with a lovely red silk sari. They walked up to the center of the bridge over a tributary of the Ganges, howling like dogs but with perfectly straight faces. Pretty soon a crowd came out from town and walked silently up to the body, then they all howled; and after an appropriate interval the body was chucked in the river. Huge turtles live in the river and eat the bodies. Supposedly the turtles are also sacred, and hygienically speaking I guess they are, as the village does its washing and gets its water from the same river.

We climaxed the trip by running out of gas some 16 miles from Gaya. No other traffic on the road and nothing to do but hoof it. Two captains started out walking. No word three hours later so I started with the other two captains. A bus passed, but it was going the wrong way and burned charcoal! No telephones of course or gas stations. After hiking about three miles I saw a car coming and stopped it. Leaning in, I said to the Indian passenger, "Do you understand English, by any chance?"

"Oh, yes," came back a perfectly cultivated English accent. He spoke it far better than we did, and turned out to be Deputy Magistrate of Gaya. Luckily, he had some extra gas and let us have it, so we arrived here about the same time as the guys who had walked, much to their annoyance!

My DFC (Distinguished Flying Cross) arrived. Got two swell letters from Nance and Dad, and found a note from Townie, who got transferred to Tezpur so we could be together. Slightly ironic!

Red Cross canteen, the only good thing here, was closed today! No reason given. The motorcycles, which guys went to great length to get have, been banned! Thieriot and I are weeping on each other's shoulders, he more than me as he's still a second lieutenant.

We fired my bearer, and the one I have now is worse still. Mice and rats all over the place. Plague will probably start next! The rats are almost as big as cats and will eat anything left around – cookies, candies, etc. The hunting party between classes bagged one antelope and five green parrots, both species being very good eating but not what they were looking for. Thieriot and Tutt went and didn't get anything but sore feet.

Oct. 9-17 – By hard fighting for planes I'm now only 90 hours from going home, some three times the amount I was supposed to get when I came down here a month ago. Nothing like Gaya retrogression!

Had four Tezpur guys I knew in last two classes, and got all but one through. Had to wash out one guy, and now he's spread the story that I'm a rough character to have as an instructor. I probably was with him, as I thought he'd kill us both before we were through.

Went to Benares in between classes with Thieriot, Tutt, Galloway and Higginbotham, all lieutenants, and we had a swell time. It's the Holy City of India for the Hindus, and there are no white people living there at all except at the British Army camp. We stayed at a hotel there and got a guide to steer us around. Besides being the Holy City, it's also the center of the brass industry and brocade weaving, and they really make beautiful stuff, even if it is Indian. Bought a brass jigger, a brass idol of Gonesh, the elephant-headed god of good luck, a small ivory figure, and some material for an evening jacket for Nance.

In the morning we went down to the Ganges, which is undoubtedly the filthiest river I ever saw. The Indians "bathe" in it to cleanse themselves of sin, and don't seem to care if they wade in with or without their saris on. There was a yogi standing motionless on a platform on one leg with the other one doubled up by his hip in some manner, and he stayed that way by the **day**, not the hour.

The burning ghats where the bodies are cremated are there, and we saw a woman burn. They place the body in the river for several hours to get it thoroughly soaked in "holiness," then put it on the logs, put more on top, and the nearest relative, in this case the husband, brings the fire from the temple and starts the cremation. In the old days, if a man dies, his favorite wife would throw herself on his pyre to burn along with him, but the British stopped that. The young kids under five are thrown into the river for the turtles!

The Hindus believe that anyone who dies there and is burned, and his ashes strewn in the river, will be reincarnated in a higher plane of life, so the old and feeble come from all over India, and if they die on the way someone brings them in anyhow. Their whole life is bound up in religion and based on this rebirth idea, which is lucky, because if a guy gets born into the lower classes, such as the two divisions of the outcasts, he can never better himself and is worse off than a medieval varlet.

The streets were crowded with filth all draining into the river, as well as camels, pigs, dogs, cows, chickens, goats and millions of natives, and each little alley in the shopping center is devoted to a trade, such as "The Street of the Brass Makers," which literally glittered with reflected light from the brassware they had spread out on white cloths in the little stalls. Hig and I objected to buying at the places where the guide took us as we knew he would be getting a commission out of what we bought, so we split off and found our own little shop up a dirty alley and up a flight of stairs. We argued and bargained and finally bought after threatening to leave twice, and when we were all through, everyone grinning happily, we discovered that he'd come down a lot but we had still paid more than the place the guide took us to!

At the hotel a native was there with a series of little baskets, with cobras, gopher snakes, grass snakes and kraits, and two little bags for a big and little mongoose. He charmed the cobras, which looked vicious, hissed and raised their hoods to strike, but after we'd made a deal and the mongoose had fought and killed one, we discovered its fangs had been taken out and the poison removed. But brother those Rikk-Tikki-Tavi's are fast! The most interesting thing was that the native handled them all easily and carelessly, except for the kraits, which he picked up only by the tail and with a quick jerk.

On the way back, a native with a bear on a leash and a muzzle put on a show where the bear danced. It danced all night and so would I if I was in his spot, as a string had been strung through a hole in his snout and every time the native yanked it, it hurt! The bear would jump and howl and toddle around on his hind feet.

Bad news when we got back. Townie went down on his first trip over the Hump. He was with Maclean who had bailed out with Haynie in China last June. This time they were empty and in 590, my ship the Nancy P., and they bailed out over Shinbwi-yang, where I had my emergency landing. They haven't been found, when last I heard, but if they got out of the ship OK I'd stack Townie and Mac against even **that** jungle any day. Will try to go to Tezpur after this class and get more dope.

The Diary
Part 6

Oct. 17-Nov. 15 — I've finally finished my time and argued the sergeant in the records division not to try to find any more time for me to fly, but to send my name in for rotation! I have hopes now for being home in time for Christmas!!

The flying has been pretty uneventful, as all instructing is. However, I've been on three test hops and they've been more than exciting. On the first, the ship vibrated so much that Parker and I felt we'd have to bail out, but we fixed that. On the second I lost an engine just as the wheels left the ground. It wouldn't feather, and when I cut off the power and looked out to see that we weren't on fire, I saw the other engine losing all its oil and getting ready to quit. Just got it around, and after taking off east landed south before I lost the other engine on the right side. On the third, we had a runaway prop on takeoff!

All the October recommendations for promotions were returned! The valley promotions are now open and the boys at Tezpur are all getting them. In fact, by now with the exception of Stafford, they've all gotten their promotions and gone home!

No word from Townie. Apparently he either got hurt landing and didn't survive, or his chute never opened. According to Maclean, who is OK, as are the others of the crew, Mac was the last out of the ship. They were on instruments about 30 miles east of Shinbwiyang. Mac says he saw three chutes open, but he was on instruments and in a terrific hurry to get free in time for his chute to open. By Mac's order they all went out the top hatch instead of the rear door though the ship was empty. That was the worst mistake he made as there is danger of getting caught or hit on the tail of the ship when leaving through the top hatch, and no danger from the rear door. However, Mac had bailed out through the top hatch before, and I guess he figured it was the best way. Apparently they got water in the gas when refueling at Chengtu and all four engines quit on them.

Somerville and his crew crashed on landing the other day. He was coming back empty with an engine feathered, overshot and went around, and on the second approach the other engine on the same side quit. He swerved off to one side, tried to belly it up in a rice paddy, but the cabin hit a bunch of trees. The copilot is OK, the engineer was killed, and the two radio operators have fractured skulls.

Bill Houston and Beane are long overdue with no word of them. They left empty from Chengtu. Heusley, a Jorhat boy whom I had for a couple of periods here, went in on takeoff from Jorhat, and Mohanbari and Sookerating have lost about 12 ships.

The boys don't have either the training or experience they used to. Proctor and Butow down fatally, and probably more, and until then we'd gone eight months with no losses. June was about when the old instruction system went out and the new grads started coming over. They just haven't got the flying experience, that's all.

Hank Tutt and I are going on leave for ten days to Srinagar,

Kashmir, and hope to have our orders when we get back. Plan to go home by way of Cairo, Casablanca and by boat from there! Pittsburgh is where I get my orders from, and as that's only an ATC gas stop, they should be pretty willing to help out.

Went out to Bud Gaya, the temple outside of town which is the source of Buddhism, and got a special tour with Dorcas Dunklee, the Red Cross girl. Apparently Buddha sat under a bow tree and started his religion by sitting for seven years contemplating his navel!

The horse deal fell through as we were flying night and day through the fair, but all the decent horses sold for about 2,500 rupees anyhow. Went to town with Dorcas to look for curtains for the club and ended up ordering three elephants for a Thanksgiving party, a gymkhana affair, and buying some silk for Nance! Still have nothing for Dad or Bud or the kids.

The election is over and FDR is in again. I hope he lasts so Truman won't get near the presidency. I'm sorry FDR is still in power, but I must admit Dewey was no bargain. The greatest loss this country has was Wendell Wilkie's death! He was a great man and a great leader.

The war is going pretty good, thank Heaven. I should think the Germans would collapse about next June and the Japs by the end of next year! Now that we're in the Philippines maybe they can stop this damn Hump operation and go for seaports in China proper.

Nov. 16-Dec. 17 – A whole month gone by and I'm on my way home waiting for a boat, of all things. Hank and I went on leave and enjoyed ourselves immensely, though we never got as far as Srinagar. We stayed at Lahore, an English settlement outside of an old native village on the route to Kashmir. We couldn't get in the good hotel (which cramped our style considerably) but we had hot water for a tub and a great barn of a room. The city was reasonably clean, though not as good as Delhi, and had four or five nightclubs. We teamed up with Pete Nissen and Sid Cave, two Aussie RAF boys with broad accents who had been flying out of Imphal in DC-3's dropping supplies to the troops fighting around Fiddim. Sid was through and on vacation before going back to Australia, but Pete had been transferred with his squadron apparently for training for a paratrooper movement on Rangoon!

We bicycled all over, drank together, played golf and admired the other guys' technique in picking up the Anglos. The boys finally got some dates for themselves, but I guess I lived too long in the south. They all looked black to me.

Met a very nice English family with two attractive daughters who were on their way home after seven years over here. Lorna, the oldest, had been a nurse, a musician, a dentist's aid, an AWVS and a teacher, and still felt at loose ends. The younger, Carol, had been engaged to an American officer who had died the day before the engagement was to be announced! They all hated "Limeys," surprisingly enough, as they were all very "Limey" themselves.

Hank, Pete, Sid and I went to the races and had a swell time taking pictures of the pure Indian girls, who were lovely in their silver and gold saris, and trying to figure out which horse was the one who had been fixed to win the race. All the races were openly acknowledged to be fixed!

Bought a sari, some fur gloves, two wooden boxes and a small sapphire. Had a very funny trip by train back consisting of trying to stay warm wrapped up in our coats and trying to keep more than five people out of a compartment for four. Indian trains are really the worst imaginable. There's no heat, no food, no blankets or covering, and they all carry twice as many people as they were built for.

Stopped in Delhi for a day where I picked up two pocketbooks, a small fur hat and tried to talk Hank into buying a fur coat – stone marten – **only three hundred dollars**.

Went on to Agra and had my first glass of milk and had Thanksgiving dinner there. It was pretty good. Arrived back at Gaya to find that Parker had gotten his name sent in 50 hours before he was through and had gotten special orders the minute he was finished. Hank and Grif and I didn't come out on the orders on the 1st, so the Colonel sent a wire to find out why, and Grif went to Calcutta to see. Apparently Beaver had tried to foil us again and had sent a message not to release us!

Also discovered that despite contrary promises, no one had been put in for a promotion. Col. Mann, the Executive Officer, sent a letter to the General for me, but it won't do any good.

Got our orders despite Beaver on the 8th. Grif, Tutt and I left that night and arrived in Karachi the next morning. Got orders out that night and left for Cairo via Abidan, Iran, after buying two small ivory perfume bottles.

Cairo is paradise! We didn't get into town, but the reports make it sound like being stationed at Los Angeles or Houston. Met a couple more Milwaukee boys. They are almost all over here now.

Went on in two days to Casablanca via Tripoli and Oran. A long rough trip in bucket seats, colder than the devil and a bad pilot. We've been here for five days waiting for transportation and have spent our time vainly trying to get on ships as extra crew members or to fly a war-weary plane home. Today we heard we go by ship, which means we can't make Christmas at home. Very annoying as Grif and I had arranged to take a B-17 home and had it swiped from under our noses by Captains Brown, Pawley and Fletcher here as well as Powell from Tezpur and Weiss from Milwaukee. The former are all going back with us but Weiss has that tough run between here and Cairo with three-day layovers at each end.

Spent our time trying to keep warm in a tent and going to town to buy some Moroccan leather. Finally got a hassock, a purse, and four wallets! My bag looks like Santa Claus! And Heaven knows what the duty will be.

Casa only misses Humphrey Bogart to make it perfect. The people range from immaculate 2nd Lieutenants to drunken Majors and G.I.s, free French sailors, CBI boys all looking pretty bad, Mohammedans with and without veils, camels, donkeys, buses, airplanes, dog carts, women of all kinds but mostly the wrong kind, and beggars.

The cafes are thronged with this motley group all drinking bad wine out of horrible green glasses unwashed since 1930, I think. And the streets are crammed with bands of kids begging, stealing and "rolling" you. Two G.I.'s were found the other night without their heads! One never goes around alone at night, not only from fear of robbers, but from fear of getting lost or picked up by some guy masquerading as a soldier!

At the moment there are some 500 Number 4 Priority passengers backlogged. All Americans – the Navy, the British, the Poles, the Canadians, the Russians and the French all travel Numbers 2 or 3 on our airlines! All going west to battle assignments, so they say. I'm damned if I knew we were fighting the Germans or the Japs in the States!

There is nothing like the philanthropy of America. We fight to save India for the British (or Africa or England, etc.), and we not only do that without charge, but we pay them for bases to fight from, build them ourselves after renting the land, pay a 20% royalty to the British government on all people we hire to help us, and after we're through with the bases and then have them in A-1 condition, we give them back. This is true all over India and England, Australia and the Middle East.

In China, where the 14th Air Force is the only available fighting group, we pay the Chinese for the use of these bases and give them equipment and even outfit the warlords, most of whom are fighting against us. In Burma we do the same thing besides training and equipping the Chinese who help. In France there are five American armies and one British, the latter made up of Canadians, Aussies and New Zealanders.

Dec. 17-26 – On leave I ran into a Lieutenant Biebold who was the officer who looked for Townie. Apparently they spent more time looking for him than they ordinarily did as he had some good friends in Chabua. The lieutenant parachuted into the jungle twice, the first time picking up the radio operator who was in a native village and the engineer who was lost and exhausted in the jungle and almost dead. He brought them out after searching unsuccessfully for a week for Townie, and then on the basis of a report that a chute had been seen from the air, he went in again.

The chute had gone and he believes Townie was killed landing and the natives buried him and the chute while denying all knowledge of it so they wouldn't be implicated. He said there wasn't much possibility that Townie was a prisoner in Jap hands as there were only a few patrols up there, and they wouldn't take prisoners.

Houston apparently was killed with his crew when they crashed at Chunking, and the rumor is that some of the load of Chinese soldiers he had were actually Jap saboteurs. It's perfectly possible.

Peter Dominick was one of thousands of troops who returned home on the USS West Point. (Wikimedia Commons photo)

They flew us back to Oran from Casablanca and we are on the S.S. West Point going home - Fletcher, Tutt, Griffith, Parker, Brown, Pawley, Major Phillips and myself. There are about 650 Army officers and G.I.'s, and 1,000 sailor passengers as well as the crew. The ship is big but pitches a lot, and the food is excellent.

Naturally we didn't get home for Christmas and I'm rooming with a bunch of 1st Lieutenants, one of whom graduated in 44-A, returning from combat in Italy, Burma and China. We're headed for Norfolk and then home!

The boat is nice from a food and rest point of view, but I much prefer the motion and speed of a plane! Landed at 1400 after getting up at 0400, and was herded onto a troop train.

Even American fog looks good, and the band playing as we debarked really hit us in our softest and probably best parts.

– HOME –

Editor's note: He finally received his promotion to Captain on July 29, 1945, having served as a 1st Lieutenant for 16 months.

"The Rock Pile"
Based on a Flyer's Diary

By Lt. Peter H. Dominick

India - 1944

Dane stirred uneasily and wondered what had awakened him. Robbins talking in his sleep, or just indigestion? It was too soon to go out again, or so he hoped. It couldn't be more than midnight now.

"Lieutenant Moore," a voice said insistently. A flashlight beam was shining in his face.

"What now? I'm sleeping, for Christ's sake!"

"China flight," said the CQ, pulling the mosquito net up and shoving a clipboard with a roster of names at Dane.

"Christ, not again," Dane grumbled, initialing the roster next to his name. "What are they trying to do, raise the graph again?"

Grunting in disgust and glancing quickly at the copilot's name listed under his on the roster, he swung his feet to the floor. Wonder who Bolaski is, he thought. Must be one of the new guys. Probably can't even work a radio. Sure wish some of those bastards in headquarters with their feet on the desk would start getting some more real pilots up here.

As the CQ stepped quietly out the door, Dane stumbled over to the chair where it seemed only minutes before he had dropped his flying clothes in a pile. One by one, he pulled on his woolen underwear, heavy long socks, khaki uniform and flying coveralls while sweat streamed down his face and chest. Using his flashlight, he examined the rest of the equipment: heavy fleece-line boots, pants and coat, a light leather jacket with his own insignia on it. Then he grabbed his Musette bag, which was filled with four cases of beer, some extra .45 caliber ammunition, a can of fruit juice, two packs of cigarettes, a few handkerchiefs, a free flow-and-demand type oxygen mask, a pair of wool-lined gloves, an E-625 computer, and a styptic pencil.

The latter he had carried ever since he had been to the rest camp and had been covered with jungle leeches. He had gotten them off by touching them with a lighted cigarette, but found that the wounds wouldn't stop bleeding except with a very powerful astringent. That experience, as well as the story he'd heard about the Ghurka Patrol that had taken a new route one day while fighting the Japs in Burma and had literally been eaten alive by the leeches, had convinced him that something had to be carried for emergencies.

Strapping his .45 into the shoulder holster and grabbing a flashlight, he stepped out on the porch of the basha and looked around the area. Only one other basha had its light on, and he could hear the rowdy and confused mumble of guys playing poker and drinking. "Lucky damn guys," he muttered, without animosity.

Pouring some water out of a gallon can he had swiped from the Mess Hall into the tin wash basin plainly marked "Made in Japan," he sloshed it over his face and stumbled onto the road where the shuttle truck from Operations would pick him up.
Three other men were already there. He flashed his light on them briefly and muttered, "Hi Goody, Cooper, Young. Any of you guys know Bolaski?"

"Nope," they grunted in unison, and all settled into sleepy silence again.

"When did you get in, Dane?" Cooper asked.

Dane glanced at his watch, which showed 11:30 PM. "Right after you, I guess. I landed about 14 hundred hours."

Young stirred slightly from his Indian squat and murmured, "They're getting to be in too damn much of a hurry down there. Don't know about you, but I'm still tired. Don't guess I got more than four hours sleep."

The others nodded, their cigarettes lighting up the dark like red fireflies. A 6x6 truck rumbled noisily around the corner and stopped while the four men heaved their bags on and climbed in with a nod to the other crew members already on board.

Dane stood up, holding on to the steel top ribs, and looked at the sky for a minute. Lightning was flashing vividly in all directions. Doesn't look so hot, he thought, closing his eyes and reveling in the breeze stirred up by the moving truck. He could taste the salty drip of sweat from his upper lips. Who the hell is Bolaski?! Wonder how much flying time he has. If he's another one of these kids just out of flying school I'll really be fed up.

The big truck ground to a stop by the long, low Operations Building. The four pilots trudged into the building and leaned over the counter, rubbing both sleep and dust out of their eyes. "What gives?" demanded Goody. "You guys run out of pilots, or are you conducting a new experiment to see how many hours we can go without sleep?"

Using an already damp sleeve, the Operations Officer, whose nametag read Blacker, swabbed the sweat from his forehead and chose to ignore the remark. Instead he asked, "When did you guys get in?"

"About eight hours ago," Young answered, and Dane added, "This will make my fourth night trip this week."

"Sorry fellas," Blacker said. "You're first on the list to go. All the rest came in after you except for Marlowe, and he's too drunk to move, much less fly."

Dane glared at Blacker and asked, "Who the hell is Bolaski?

I understand he's going with me."

Blacker flushed slightly. "He's a new guy. Tall, red haired - seems OK to me."

"Has he got any 4-engine time?" demanded Dane.

"Beats the shit out of me, Lt.," Blacker responded. Then, in a noncommittal voice, he added, "All you guys are going to A-3, and your ships will be ready in about a half-hour. Better get some coffee and get ready."

The four turned and started out the door. Cooper paused for a minute to scan the weather reports from the pilots who had just come back.

"Thunderstorms in the valley increasing. First Ridge socked in. No top at 22,000 feet. Burma - broken with heavy clear ice in clouds, and poor radio reception. Hump - solid overcast and ice from 15,000 feet. China - broken with front between Yunnanyi and Ipin. Winds variable, mostly from 230 degrees at 50 miles per hour."

"Sounds normal," commented Young as Cooper read it off. "C'mon, let's get some coffee and then worry about it."

Silently they slogged through the heavy night air and thick mud to the Mess Hall.

"Any more news on Newhall?" Goodie asked.

"Nope," replied Dane. "I checked just before hitting the sack and the last report from him was over Tare Jig coming back. That was early last night. Probably blew up - or some bright young Chinese lad with lots of Japanese dough put water in his gas. If that happened, he'd probably lose all four engines over the main Hump, in the middle of the soup where his radio wouldn't work. At that, I'd rather have him blow up than go down over Jap territory near Myitkyina. Those goddamn Burmese would probably do to him what they did to Baker."

"What did they do to Baker?" Young asked.

"That was before your time?"

"Yeah, I guess it must have been," Young replied.

Dane cleared his throat and looked down at the ground as he began to respond. "He went down about where Warazup is

Flying the Hump

now. They all bailed out in fine shape and made contact with the natives, as per orders. Baker gave them all the rupees in his money belt and promised more if they would help. The natives stripped them all of their clothing and Jungle Pack equipment and starved them for three days. Then they turned them over to the Japs, who had paid them more money. The Japs shot them all and broadcast the whole story the next day."

They sat sipping coffee while Young mumbled, "The bastards. The dirty bastards."

Suddenly the door banged open and a tall red-haired kid, skinny with a narrow face, bounced into the room.

"Any of you guys named Moore?" he asked.

"That's me," Dane answered. "You're Bolaski? Going with me?"

"You betcha, laddie!" grinned Bolaski, sticking out his hand and churning Dane's like a pump handle.

Dane looked at him quizzically, then waved a hand at the bench, saying, "Have some coffee before we get our chutes."

Bolaski sat down with a hop and sputtered excitedly, "How does it look?"

"Not so bad," said Dane. "Some ice reported. Don't like the damn ice."

"I can't see why everyone thinks this route is so tough," Bolaski exclaimed. "Hell, I've seen much worse weather than this in the States."

Dead silence filled the room. Then Cooper said softly, "How many trips you had?"

"Four," replied Bolaski. "We flew some instruments, but it wasn't particularly rough. The main trouble we had was making a simple instrument let-down. The guy I was with seemed to be nervous all the time and never even tried to use a range let-down."

"Where was that?" asked Dane.

"I dunno. At A-1, I think he called it."

"There isn't any range there."

"Oh," Bolaski replied in an unabashed but surprised voice.

They all got up and stumbled back through the mud, sweating more than ever from the hot coffee.

"Our planes should be ready pretty soon," Dane remarked. "You'd better get your chute and money belt. I'll meet you in the Briefing Room and we can work out our flight plan."

Bolaski galloped away, with an "Okey Dokey" thrown over his shoulder, and Cooper muttered, "Why in the hell do these guys think they know everything when they're not even dry behind the ears?"

"Oh, it's natural, I guess," said Goodie, shrugging his shoulders. "They hear all the lurid tales guys like Wild Bill Hickock get off, and they expect every trip to be like a circus, with them as spectators. At least most of them," he qualified, glancing down the porch at Bolaski, who was hopping up and down like a little boy trying not to go to the bathroom.

Dane said nothing, but went into the Operations Building and started signing his Load Manifest. What a nifty explosion this would make, he thought grimly. 2,350 gallons of gas in the wings and another 1,200 in the fuselage. The poor old buggy would go higher than a Fourth of July rocket.

Gross takeoff weight 60,000 pounds - check.

"Guess I better go in and see how that moron Bolaski is making out with the flight plan," he said.

He walked into the Briefing Room and while checking over the latest report on Jap positions, heard the Operations Officer call out, "Captain Cooper? You're all set. The truck's outside to take you out to your ship."

We're next, Dane thought, and quickly ran over the flight plan Bolaski had drawn up, making several changes in elapsed time between checkpoints, quickly feeling in the knee pocket of his coveralls for his home-made course and distance data on several different routes.

The two men walked out on the porch, Bolaski chattering gaily about something which Dane didn't bother to listen to as he looked around for his radio operator.

"All set Cushman," he said to the short dark sergeant sitting on the bench. "Better get your IFF ready, and we'll pick you up in the truck."

"OK Lieutenant," Cushman said, heading off into the dark toward another thatch-roofed building.

Dane looked at the sky again. It was black, a shining black like a quiet pool in a New England cedar grove, but the air seemed heavy and dead. Lightning striped the sky in all directions, and a continuous murmur of thunder rumbled like the muffled roar of surf.

The truck bounced over the road and up the steel mesh mat toward a revetment. Dane told the driver that they were looking for 590, and after a short jouncing ride the driver swung his truck up close to the nose of the converted B-24.

"Cushman, will you put our chutes and bags up in the cockpit? Bolaski and I will check her over."

"How is she?" Dane demanded of his Crew Chief, whose head stuck up out of the top hatch while the Radio Operator passed up their equipment.

"All OK, Captain. One generator out, and that's all."

"Thanks for the promotion, Chief," Dane said, grinning. "I've been looking for that for a long time."

Bolaski grinned and asked, "When did you get out of school?"

"Class of 42-E," Dane replied. "Check the turbo and the Zeus fasteners on the other side, will you, and I'll get this side and the nose wheel."

While they were checking the plane, a C-46 landed and taxied toward Operations.

"The rest of the valley must be closed in," muttered Dane, and then he stuck his thumb up in the Chinese good luck sign as Cooper's C-87 taxied by.

"All set over here," he called to Bolaski. "If your side's OK, let's get started."

Bolaski came around, nodding that everything checked out, and the two men clambered into the cabin through the rear hatch and skimmed past the load of gas drums.

"Tanks safetied, Chief?"

"Yup."

"2,350 gallons?"

"2,450," corrected the Crew Chief.

"Good. We may need it if everything's socked in."

The two men took their seats, and after running his eyes over the cockpit briefly, Dane nodded. Bolaski stuck his head out of the bull's eye window and called out, "Clear!"

One by one the big engines roared to life. Dane called the tower for taxi instructions. "Nan 6 Love ready for takeoff," he heard Cooper say over the radio. The tower told Cooper to stand by, and gave Dane his instructions.

Swinging sharply to the right onto the steel mesh taxi strip, 590 moved along, bouncing its nose up and down from the braking action, like a duck dipping for food. They were facing the runway when the tower gave Cooper his clearance. The big ship lurched down the runway, gaining speed as it roared by them.

As Dane watched, he exclaimed, "My God, they're too close to the end of the runway! Pull up! Pull up!"

At seemingly the last possible second, the plane lunged into the air and the gear started coming up. It brushed through the top of the bushes and flew straight out, slowly, appearing to gain altitude by mere inches. They watched it carefully until the dull glow from the turbos disappeared into the clouds, and Dane sighed with relief.

"Guess they're OK now. That was close!"

"What the hell was the matter with them?" Bolaski demanded, his voice high-pitched and dry. "Why didn't he get her off sooner?"

"I'm not sure," Dane replied, "but I think he had the 'Sad Sack' with the new electric turbos. For some reason she doesn't seem to get the same power on takeoff."

They taxied down the runway and swung around for warm up. One by one, they checked the engines and completed the rest of the items on their pre-flight check list.

"How much time does Number One have on it, Chief?" Dane

asked.

"450 hours, Lieutenant, but she seemed OK on the last flight."

"Call the tower and tell them we're ready for takeoff," he told Bolaski.

"Stand by, Mike Nine. Nan 6 Love coming in for emergency landing," the tower replied.

Dane cut the engines back and craned his neck out the window to try to pick up Cooper's lights.

"That goddamned ship," he muttered.

Suddenly through the clouds, Cooper's ship appeared, about five hundred feet off the ground, with the engines obviously straining.

Bolaski shouted, "He's coming in for a downwind landing! Number 4 is feathered!"

Cooper's ship started down the final approach, with his flaps at 50 percent and the landing gear coming down.

"Nice work," Dane breathed quietly. Suddenly he shouted, "Christ!"

Cooper's Number 3 engine had failed, and he swerved violently to the right toward the tower and the taxi strip. Slowly, the right wing came up as the power to the other two engines was yanked off. The ship settled fast, its gear brushing the roof of the tower.

Cooper desperately tried to guide the ship back toward the runway, thatch streaming in all directions from the roof of the tower and fire licking out from the cowling of the Number 3 engine. The ship hit the ground just to the right of the runway and rolled toward the trees.

"He can't stop! He can't possibly stop," Bolaski yelled. Suddenly the ship veered to the right as the two right engines were powered up and full right brake and rudder applied. The landing gear gave way, and in a cloud of mud and water the ship skidded along on its belly and wing. Smoke was rising ominously from the bad engine when the ant-like figures of the crew clambered out of the top hatch and along the wing toward safety.

Trucks started for them but swerved off at the frantic arm signals from Cooper, who threw himself on the ground. As he did so, a tremendous roar burst out and the plane virtually disintegrated before their eyes. Huge flames leaped up and licked at the sky like the angry fingers of Satan.

Dane murmured, "Beautiful job. Cooper's good, all right. By all laws, he and the crew should be six feet under right now."

Turning to Bolaski, he added, "If anything goes wrong with us, don't touch the feathering button. I'll do all that. Just do what I tell you, and do it quickly."

Bolaski nodded, for the first time completely sobered.

Dane glanced back. "All set Chief? You get the gear when I call for it."

"OK Lieutenant," answered the Chief.

The tower called, "Item Mike 9, cleared for takeoff. Climb to 18,500 and fly the Easy Course clearing Tare Victor at 10,000."

"Roger," Dane replied. "Half flaps, turbos set, mixtures auto rich, booster pumps on, generators on. Here we go again."

Through the glare cast by the burning ship to their left, the C-87 roared down the runway. 80, 90, 100, 110, and Dane could sense Bolaski tightening up beside him, and knew he must be getting pretty close to the end of the runway. 115 and the ship felt lighter. Dane eased back on the wheel just a little, and the ship gently left the runway and cleared the bushes at the end by just a few feet.

Dane's right thumb jerked up, and the engineer shoved the gear handle into the "retract" position. His eyes flicked from the gyro horizon to the airspeed indicator, the rate of climb and the altimeter. He reduced power, and banked gently left to take up his course.

"Check for gas siphoning and for leaky drums," he instructed the Chief.

The Chief came back and nodded OK, as Dane pulled out a cigarette. "Anyone who wants to smoke better do it now. No smoking while we're on oxygen."

Cushman smiled. Each pilot had his own phobias, and he

had flown enough with Dane to know that one.

The plane was already in the soup at 500 feet, with the Bramaputra River and its green tea plantations completely enshrouded. At 1,500 feet, Dane turned the ship over to Bolaski and pulled out his oxygen equipment, while watching the instruments carefully to see what kind of pilot Bolaski was. Fair enough, he thought, as the ship wobbled slightly but continued its steady climb.

"We'll fly in half hour shifts," he added aloud. "If it's too rough to handle from the right seat, I'll take over, but if not you'd better get some practice in."

Bolaski grinned eagerly and started to sing *Oh the Eagles They Fly High In Mobile.*

I must be getting old, Dane thought, as he watched Bolaski exuding enthusiasm and energy - or maybe it's this damn climate and food. Wouldn't it be wonderful to be back in the States with Nancy! Let's see, it's midnight here and noon there. Right now we'd be on vacation in Maine somewhere, probably swimming in the lake and wondering if we had sufficient ambition to fish or paddle down the slough in the afternoon. It would be cold in the water, hot in the sun, and Nancy would be slim and tan, with her auburn hair and hazel eyes gleaming. Funny how you know you'll miss a person before you go and never ever really know what it means till you've been gone a few months!

Wonder what the kids are like now, he thought, continuing his thought process. This damn war sure messes up a life. At that, I guess we've been lucky. Nance and I were together at every post in the States, and that's more than most couples can say. Mike must be beginning to walk, and Dane Jr. is probably already swimming. Well, he silently wished, it shouldn't be too much longer before I'll be home again. This must be about my 55th trip, with only about twenty more to go. That is, IF I make it. What a laugh all that education I got was. Private school, college, law school - 24 years of it, and I can't see that it helped much except to get enjoyment out of good books and perhaps to make friends more easily.

The plane lurched sharply and Dane glanced at Bolaski. The sweat was beginning to dry on his face, his hands tightened on the wheel. Another sharp bounce came and Dane called, "I've got it. Put on your mask and heavy jacket."

Almost without thinking, Dane controlled the big ship as it lurched through the clouds, skidding around like butter on a warm plate. His thoughts continued to roam: We certainly look like Wells' concept of the men from Mars, with their heavy boots, coats, pants and masks. I wonder whether death is so bad. Maybe it's something like this. Flying through blackness into blackness, and away from blackness. No sun, no clouds, no earth, no trees, nothing but silent figures and blackness. If we could just accept it, it would be so much easier. Just fly and fly and fly like automatons, and after a while the ship, the engines, the people, knowledge itself would fall into black nihilism, and everything would dissolve. Sure, that would be easy, but not nearly as interesting as I'd hope for. It would be wonderful to meet all the famous people of centuries past, to be able to talk to them, to find out what kind of a person John the Baptist was. What happens when John and Napoleon meet? Do they tip hats and pass by without speaking, like Mr. Ames and Mr. Duncan used to do at home after their wives had fought at a bridge game? How do Washington and Lincoln get along? Does the Virginia planter recognize the backwoodsman, or do they look at problems from two completely different viewpoints? Maybe there aren't any problems. That would be too dull; too much like the Mohammedan Nirvana where the men lie on cushions and get fed young girls and sweetmeats.

Probably Bolaski would question my sanity for thinking about stuff like this, and maybe he's right. But Dane couldn't help letting his mind wander among his gardens of memories and the possible paths of his future, or lack of one; and unbidden, his thoughts returned to his bride, the love of his life.

That afternoon with Nancy on their wedding trip had been one for the ages. The small cottage in the Catskills, cut off from all the neighbors, with the sun beating down on the bank of the stream below the garden. We must've been as close to being pure pagan as anyone ever was. I remember so well how we looked at each other, and the world seemed so perfect. There was no need for conversation, food or clothing.

I'll always remember Nance, turning slightly, pressing against me as I untied the knot on her ridiculously small bandana bra, and slid it off. Lying on the bank, gently moving my hands over her warm velvety skin and feeling her breasts tighten like rosebuds under my fingers. The universe seemed to be part of us. For ages we lay in the sun, exploring each other and our love with all our senses. Shivers of excitement and delight tightened our skin until finally, surrounded by the tall trees rustling their leaves with little echoes of applause, we blended together and became one for all time. God it was wonderful. Clean, beautiful and natural. And when we were tired, we slid into the brook and played together like children. Will we ever be able to get back to that again? Will the strain, fatigue and separation make us strangers again? Damn this war!

A vivid flash of lightning momentarily blinded him and cut his daydream short. "Cockpit lights on," he ordered, pulling his mask aside momentarily.

Bolaski stared at him and asked, "Are you going into that damn mess?"

"Any other suggestions?" grinned Dane.

"We could turn around and go back."

"You get court-martialed for that," Dane replied quietly. "By order of the Iron Cheese, anyone who turns around because of weather will be court martialed," he recited in a singsong voice. Lightning crashed against the wing, and a greenish blue ball of fire rolled along it. Bolaski jumped nervously, and looked out, expecting the wing to part company with the fuselage. But nothing happened. A faint shiver crept over the plane.

Here we go again, Dane thought, glancing quickly at his altimeter, which showed 18,500 feet. Suddenly the airspeed started dropping off, and the plane settled. 150, 145 ... Dane increased the power and pointed the nose down. Still the airspeed dropped. 140 ... Dane shoved the wheel down farther and kept his hand on the throttle. The plane was now descending at a rate of 1,550 feet per minute and barely holding an airspeed of 145.

Suddenly Dane felt a slight change in the controls. They seemed to bite into the air, and automatically he cut back on the power. His altitude was 16,700 feet, and the rate of climb still showed the plane losing altitude, but the airspeed started to pick up. He kept his eyes flicking between the gyro horizon and the airspeed indictor. Suddenly the airspeed shot to 170. He cut back still more on the throttle and increased the rpms to keep the engines from cooling off too rapidly.

180. Dane looked at the rate of climb and saw they were going up 2,000 feet per minute, and the airspeed was increasing. His hand dropped on the gear lever, and with a rushing roar of wind, the wheel doors opened and the plane slowed down slightly.

The altimeter now showed 20,000 feet, and they were still going up at 2,000 feet per minute. At 24,000 feet the plane leveled off and Dane retracted his gear.

He looked over at Bolaski, whose forehead dripped sweat. His mouth was shaping into an uncertain grin of relief.

He'll do, thought Dane. A few more trips and he'll see why we're glad to get off this run. He pointed to the next radio check point, and Bolaski tuned in the radio compass.

Not a squeak came out.

"Goddamnit. That lightning strike must have knocked out the radio. Now we're really in a jam. Let's see, the valley's socked in, but the guys were reporting broken clouds and thunderstorms between The Hump and A-3. Probably have a better chance busting out in the clear in China than turning back."

He slid his mask off his face momentarily and yelled to Bolaski, "Radio out. We'll have to go in by dead reckoning alone. Keep a fifteen-minute check on our estimated position on the map."

Bolaski nodded and shivered violently. It was very cold now. The outside air temperature registered -30 degrees centigrade, and Dane eased the plane down.

When it was cold and black like this, the urge to shrink into the fleece-lined coat and go to sleep was almost overpowering. He remembered how mad another copilot had gotten on one occasion when they were coming back from China, taking off at about 4:40 AM, and just as they passed over Yunnanyi and could see The Hump ahead, the sun had broken through and shown through his bulls-eye window, relaxing and warming him. The copilot and engineer were asleep, and the radio operator was halfway there. Dane had looked out and felt as though he was flying through a tremendous colored photograph. The clouds looked to him like dirty powder puffs, and up ahead The Hump had a crown of long grey hairs dyed pink on the edges from the bright rays of rising sun. Drowsily he had noticed a colored archway forming in the layer of clouds ahead, with nothing but darkness beyond it. And as they approached the archway, the darkness beyond grew somehow darker and yet softer too. Suddenly he had felt a violent shove, and jerked up to find the plane spiraling gently toward the ground. He had inadvertently dozed off, a fact not lost on his copilot, who was mouthing curses into his oxygen mask. Yes, he remembered, it's so easy to do when you're tired, and cold, and the only noise is the monotonous roar of the engines ...

For about an hour they flew straight ahead, and then, estimating that they must be over Yunnanyi, Dane turned northeast. The ship was at 18,500 feet again, and Dane knew that the minimum instrument altitude for this leg is 19,500 feet.

Glancing out the window, he noticed only a slight amount of rime ice had collected on the wings. Calling the crew chief, he instructed him to keep checking for clear ice, and then powered up the engines to climb.

At 20,000 feet, he thought, they should be clear of the mountains, unless we turned too soon. IF we did, we'll run right into those Tibetan monstrosities. I guess I'd better fly east 6 or 7 minutes more, just to be sure.

Turning east again he flew out the extra time, and then

turned back toward the northeast, on course. Lightning had begun throwing its deadly darts through the skies ahead again. That must be that front between Yunnanyi and Ipin - looks pretty bad, he thought.

Tensions were already high among the crew when a dim blue glow arced around the bottom of the propellers. Gradually it increased, until all four props had a halo of blue fire around them. Then the pitot tubes on either side of the nose of the ship began glowing, as if they were coming to life. Fingers of green fire crept up to the windows of the cockpit and ran all over them as if searching for a way inside. Streamers of green flames shot out three feet in front of the props and rolled around the windshield. St. Elmo's Fire! It was a beautiful and awe-inspiring sight. So much electricity was in the air that the hair on the back of Dane's neck prickled from it. His fingers started tensing on the wheel as he waited for the shock of the storm ahead. Suddenly all the static electricity seemed to merge into a huge ball of fire which rolled along the wing and discharged with a pop audible even above the noise of the engines. At the same moment they plunged into the violent current of the storm. The plane rocked violently from side to side, buffeted around like a toy in a giant's fingers.

Dane sat quietly, moving the controls only enough to keep the plane as level as possible, and to keep his airspeed within limits. Rain washed over the windshield in torrents as ominous crackling noises started. The whole plane started shuddering, and hail beat down like stones on a tin roof. Dane sank way down in his seat and kept his eyes glued on the instrument panel.

A large ball of ice slammed into the windshield and cracked it. Other pieces kept hitting the same spot, the way a boxer will keep targeting his opponent's eye. There was a sharp crack, and a piece of the windshield broke in, letting a torrent of rain, hail and ice cold air into the cockpit.

Just at that moment, the hail stopped, and the ship broke out over an overcast. Stars were shining. The night seemed peaceful and calm, as the ship glided over the top of the grey blanket of clouds, but it was icy cold in the ship now, and Dane knew he would have to let down pretty soon before they all froze.

Were those mountains underneath, or just clouds? How far down was the base? If they flew farther, would there be a break? Could the radio operator get anything on his set?

"Are we over Ipin yet?" he yelled to Bolaski.

"We should be," Bolaski yelled back. "But I don't know how we can be sure. We haven't had any radio contact or seen the ground in the last four hours."

"OK. We'll fly ten more minutes on this heading. If there's no break that we can go down through, we'll turn northwest toward A-1 and start letting down. And for Chrissakes put your mask on! We can't afford to have anyone passing out! You take her for a minute."

Bolaski nodded, slipping on his mask again and grabbing the wheel, his hands shaking from cold, fear and excitement.

Dane motioned the Crew Chief up.

"Check for ice. She feels awfully sluggish. After you've done that, buckle your chute and get Cushman to do the same. We'll fly on this heading for a little while longer, and then start letting down."

The Chief nodded and went back to check the tail surfaces. In a couple of minutes he returned, looked through the astro dome and told Dane, "Glaze ice on all surfaces. Not too bad now, but if we pick up much more it'll be rough. Something seems to be the matter with the leading edges of the wing and tail - probably that goddamn hail."

Silently he buckled his chute and nodded at Cushman, who did the same, his face expressionless.

Dane shrugged and looked at the cloud layer beneath them. It seemed to be receding somewhat. That should but didn't necessarily indicate that the terrain level was getting lower. He glanced at his watch and looked around. No break was visible. The crew were all shivering, and the ship just didn't feel right.

"Nothing for it but to pick up speed by letting down, I guess."

He tapped the wheel and nodded his head. Bolaski relaxed and started wiping his hands. Dane smiled and thought, I wonder what he thinks of the run now?

He eased off some power and let the ship nose down. At 19,000 feet they were skimming the top. Octopus tentacles of grey fuzz crept around them like soft smothering folds of gas. Slowly they dipped down, and once again were lost in their own private world. The plane existed. The instruments were alive. Everything else seemed to dissolve from reality. Suddenly he wondered about the instruments - were they really alive?

The altimeter wasn't moving, but their airspeed was reducing. The ship felt the same. The controls weren't sloppy. He looked again. The altimeter was motionless. The airspeed registered 120. They should be stalled, but they weren't.

Suddenly vibrations rocked the ship. He looked out at the wings, and instinctively pushed the nose down even more. Great fingers of ice projected from the cowling, and the pitot tubes were frozen solid. Ice layers were creeping back over the top edge of the wing.

Grabbing his canteen, Dane reached out and cracked the glass over the altimeter. It jumped from 19,000 to 17,500. He yelled over to Bolaski.

"Ice! Pitot tubes frozen. This gives us a vague idea of our altitude. It reads off cockpit pressure. Out of luck on airspeed. We'll let down by tower settings and gyro horizon."

Bolaski was too cold than do more than nod. If I ever get out of this, he thought, so help me, I'll never fly this goddamn rock pile again.

I hope to God we're within twenty miles of our track, Dane thought, as he watched the altimeter unwind slowly.

If we've overshot A-1, we'll be in the Tibetan district. Can't worry about that now though – we'll all be dead. Even the foothills are at 19,000 feet. And that big job I saw the other day must go over 26,000. God, won't the ice ever quit?! The poor old girl won't take much more. We should start getting below it at 12,000 feet. Wonder whether that'll be enough to clear the mountains to the south of Ipin. There's one place where they break off pretty suddenly. This business of letting down on estimated time over an unknown checkpoint is stuff for dodo birds! The altimeter showed 14,000, 13,000, 12,000 ... Dane glanced at his windshield, which was frozen solid, but the anti-icer alcohol was beginning to make an impression now - 11,000, 10,000 ... There was a loud report, causing Bolaski to jump like a skittish colt.

Dane leaned over and said, "Ice breaking off the nose section and hitting the fuselage. We should be out of the worst pretty soon. Keep your mask on until we reach 6,000 feet."

At 6,000 feet, the crew took off their masks and listened gleefully to the ice cracking off the wings and fuselage. Suddenly the airspeed started to move. It raced up to 170, and Dane reduced power slightly. Calling the crew together, he said slowly, "We don't know for sure where we are. Counting the overflying I did on the last two legs, we should be northeast of A-1 and about ten minutes out. I'm going to try to contact the tower on the command set and have them give us a bearing before we let down any further."

For fifteen minutes they circled, calling constantly, but either they were too far away or the set was not transmitting. There was no response.

Dane called the crew again.

"You can bail out now or not. I'm not going to order you to do it, but I think it's the sensible thing to do. We'll have to let down to get down under this, and letting down blind gives us less than a 50-50 chance."

"What about you, Lieutenant?" asked Cushman.

"Well," Dane replied, grinning sheepishly, "I think I know where we are. I've never cracked up a ship yet, and I think I'll take a chance on sweating it out. I admit it isn't particularly sensible, given the faulty altimeter readings."

"We'll stick," the Chief and Cushman said together.

"Hell yes," grinned Bolaski. "We've gotten this far. We might as well deliver this load of crap."

Dane nodded and straightened out on course. Slowly he started letting down. Two minutes passed, and they hit 5,000 feet. Five minutes passed and they were at 4,500, and still no break was visible. Everyone was sweating heavily.

Ten minutes passed - no one moved. They were at 4,000 feet indicated, the clouds still wrapped around them like an enchanted blanket.

"Prepare to bail out," ordered Dane.

The Crew Chief and Radio Operator stood up and fingered their chutes uneasily.

"Chief, we'll stay up here and circle for a while. You and Cushman go back and jettison the hatch door. Clear a passage by dumping some of the gas drums, and put one drum as far in the tail section as you can to balance the ship's weight. When that's done, come back.

"Bolaski, try the command set again. See if you can pick up any station at all. Call A-1 first, then keep calling and tune in on A-3, Ipin, and Kunming to see if anyone can hear us."

Dane started circling gently, his thoughts racing. *I wonder if this it? Should I jump or try a let-down? Minimum altitude is 3,500 feet west of the field, for fifteen minutes, but 2,000 is safe east of the field for about ten minutes. How accurate is this altimeter? Cabin pressure is probably higher than outside pressure, the higher the pressure the lower the reading, so I should have more altitude than indicated. I've never scratched a plane yet, and I've been in tight scrapes before. I wish I knew how far down this damn overcast goes.*

There was a sudden jar, and the plane yawed to the left. The Chief came back at a run, stammering excitedly.

"The cargo door hit the vertical fin and took most of it off. The tail is vibrating badly."

"You're telling me," Dane replied dryly. "Get the drums out quickly, Chief. I'll climb to 5,500. When they're out let me know."

The Chief went back as the plane struggled up to 5,000 feet. The rumble of gas drums going out the door could be plainly heard. In a few minutes, the Chief and Cushman made their way forward again.

"Cushman, send out a blind Mayday on the liaison set, then tie down the key. Put the IFF on Emergency. OK, you and the Chief go back and jump - Chief, you're first, and then Cushman. And hurry. I don't like the way she's acting."

The two men hurried back and stood for a moment in the door. Then they waved and jumped quickly, disappearing like ghosts in the fog.

"Bolaski, you're next."

"What are you going to do?" Bolaski asked nervously.

"I'll be right behind you," said Dane. "Getting that hole knocked into the rudder decided me. I'll probably pass you in the air. When you get down, contact the Chinese. Don't try and get to the plane again, and don't worry about me. Head west when you land. There are Japs to the east and the north. Get going now, and good luck!"

Bolaski jumped up, checked his chute and went back.

"So long, Dane. Good luck," he called, and stepped out into the murky clouds.

As he did so, the plane fell off to the left and the instruments for the Number One engine started dancing all over.

"Goddamnit! That ties the tin can on it. I can't get out now. Not with having to get my chute and myself past those barrels. Couldn't keep the plane level enough or keep enough altitude without my automatic pilot anyhow. I'll have to let down and take a long chance."

He reached up to feather the prop and discovered it wouldn't feather. Cutting off all power and watching carefully for any sign of fire, he advanced the power on the remaining engines and started letting down slowly. They had been circling so much, he had no idea where he was, so he decided to let down on a southerly heading, which he hoped would take him over the river.

4,500 feet, 4,000, 3,500, 3,000 ... still no break in the clouds. Rivers of sweat were pouring down his face, but his hands were still light on the wheel. Gingerly, he poked her nose down again.

2,500 feet, 2,400, 2,000 ... still he could see nothing but blackness. I guess I could've chanced a jump, he thought ruefully. I'll never get that altitude back now though.

1,800 feet. Suddenly he saw a flash of something underneath him and he pulled up hard, disappearing into the soup again at 2,000 feet.

Cautiously dipping down and edging toward the east, he let the ship down to 1,900 feet and turned on a landing light. The light shone down and suddenly reflected off some water. Is that the river or a rice paddy? Dane wondered desperately. There's nothing for it but to go down and see.

Letting down another hundred feet, he could dimly make out a river to the left, so he turned gently into his bad engine to follow it. I must be north of the field. The river goes past it on the left and the field is on the delta where a big tributary joins. Or is this the tributary? I'll have to find it soon. I can't float along at 300 feet for long without hitting something!

Smoke suddenly started to billow out of the bad engine. He couldn't reach the extinguisher to the right of the copilot's seat, so there was nothing to do but watch it burn.

Straining his eyes ahead for a spot to land, Dane saw a flicker of light to the right. Was it a field? It must be! He dropped half flaps, and the ship slowed down to 150. And then ahead, he saw a runway. He swerved over to the right and hit the gear handle. The gear started down, and so did the ship.

It's now or never, Dane thought grimly, as he cut off his other outboard engine and advanced the two inboards. The plane was settling fast and the end of the runway was a little far. Desperate, he threw full power to the two inboards and pulled up the nose. The plane rose up over a low tree, shuddered and dropped gently on the edge of the runway.

Shaking from nervous exhaustion, with sweat pouring down his face, he let it roll to the end, and then pulled off and cut his engines. He jumped out of his seat and ran as quickly as he could to the rear door. He leaped out just as a Jeep drove up.

"What the hell are you doing coming in without a clearance?" yelled the officer in the back seat. "Are you the pilot?"

Dane leaned back, looked at the officer and said wearily, "Oh Christ! Go dip your head in some sheep shit. What the hell do you want, an Army band?"

Suddenly he noticed that the officer was grinning. His face looked strangely familiar.

"Bolaski!" he yelled. "How the hell did you get here?"

"Floated down like a ruddy duck, me boy! Plawstered me arse on the front of Operations," Bolaski continued as he grabbed Dane by the shoulders and helped him into the Jeep. Dane grinned feebly and fell into the truck.

"We'll get the Alert Crew to move the ship, Captain," the driver said, but Dane didn't even hear the promotion. Nance, he was thinking, don't worry – I know I'll be back now.

"Good Work! You Made It Again!" said the signs over the Operations building. Dane looked at them and thought, "OK, I made it this time. But how long, Oh Lord, how long?"

Afterword

For as long as I can remember, I have been rebellious, mistrustful of authority at best, and overly sensitive. These qualities often put me at odds with my father, who ironically had similar qualities. I winced at some of his language in reading over the diary, but also laughed at the things he said about military life. I knew from having grown up with him that he also grew, rejecting racism, supporting social justice, fighting to stop the federal government's over-reach into states' affairs, and doing his best to protect and serve his beloved state of Colorado.

I am awed by the singularity of purpose that propelled him through life. That purpose, I believe, was something intrinsic to his character.

In 1982, at the celebration of his life on the day that was declared Peter Dominick Day in Colorado, the keynote speaker, then-Vice President George H. W. Bush, referred to him as a "Senator's Senator, someone who served with honor and who was greatly respected by his peers, regardless of whether or not they agreed with him."

The same is true of me. I loved him, respected him, and often disagreed with him. Mostly I did that quietly in my mind, because he also scared the living daylights out of me when he was angry.

I was the youngest child and really didn't see much of him. The first time I actually remember him was when he came back from a three-week hunting trip to British Columbia when I was three or four years old. My mother woke me from my nap and took me to the top of the stairs to say hello. Staring up at me was a very dirty, bearded man in hunting clothes, and I burst into tears.

My siblings each had different relationships with him. Peter Jr. was inspired by him, but shadowed by the burden of being the first-born son of a very famous and powerful man. Michael, who became an attorney and now holds the distinction of being the longest-serving solo law practitioner in Boulder, Colorado, admired and respected him. He told me after Dad's death that he wished he could still talk to him and ask his advice about legal issues. My sister, Lynne, also loved and respected him, in spite of having been treated differently because of her gender.

In part because of that, she became acutely aware of gender inequality and has fought for change from a very early age. Her first fight in that regard was with my parents when they brought me home from the hospital. She said, "I already have two brothers, thank you very much, so take him back and bring me a baby sister."

The family dynamic shifted dramatically when my father got into politics in 1954. My parents had settled in Colorado soon after World War II ended in 1945 and my dad joined the then-small law firm of Holland & Hart. My two oldest brothers were joined by a third, Stevie, shortly after the war, but tragedy struck and he died at two years old. A couple of years later my sister was born, and I came along in December of 1953.

My brothers were twelve-and-a-half and eleven years older than me, and were both away at school in the east before I knew how to walk and talk. When I was eight, I asked my mother if I was a mistake. She laughed and said, "No, but you were a surprise!"

This photo, likely taken in 1955, shows our entire family in Colorado. From left are my brothers, Michael and Peter Jr.; our mother, Nancy, is holding me; my sister, Lynne, is in the foreground along with our dog, Pudgy; and our father, Peter, is on the right.

My brothers benefited greatly from growing up in Colorado – riding horses, hiking, hunting, camping and fishing, learning how to be self-sufficient, and loving the abundant outdoor opportunities Colorado had to offer. I, on the other hand, moved with my parents and my sister to Washington, D.C., in January 1960, when I was barely seven years old, where my father served the Second District of Colorado in the US Congress. He ran for and won a US Senate seat in 1962 and was re-elected in 1968, but lost badly in his bid for a third term in 1974.

My sister and I split school years during most of that time, attending Colorado schools in the fall and Washington-area schools in the winter and spring. This was not my idea. I wanted to stay with my parents in Washington, but Dad was adamant. He loved Colorado and wanted Lynne and me to benefit from living there as much as Peter and Michael had.

I've told myself that he didn't understand how hard it was for us to have to have two sets of academic pressure, two sets of friends, and a wild succession of live-in babysitters to care for us while we were in Denver and our parents were in D.C.

We certainly didn't benefit from living in the state he loved in the way he intended, because he and Mom weren't around to be a part of it. I repeatedly asked Dad to let me stay a full year in Washington, and was allowed to do that in fourth grade and eighth grade. All the other years were split.

To be sure, our young lives were made interesting by the political life of Washington. I sat on my father's lap on the Senate floor when John Glenn received the Congressional Medal of Honor (the second affront to my sister's sensibilities regarding gender equality – women were not yet allowed on the Senate floor.) I had Sunday breakfast with my father and President Nixon at the White House. Lynne and I both attended the famous Easter celebration and egg roll contest on the lawn of the White House during the Kennedy administration, hosted for all the children of the members of Congress. We could smell the smoke from the riots in downtown D.C. after Martin Luther King Jr. was assassinated in 1968. We had friends at school whose fathers were cabinet secretaries, politicians, diplomats, and spies.

It seemed to me that my father had become more absent from the family. He did what he felt he had to do. He had very strong opinions about right and wrong, and had great ambitions for himself and the country he loved without reserve. My mother, who also had difficulty with his career change, nevertheless loved and supported him, always viewing that as her first priority. Being directly involved in the day-to-day of child rearing just wasn't something they did or even really knew how to do, frankly. Many of my lifelong friends have shared with me that their parents also were not hands-on in the way parents are today. There was no attending sporting events, recitals, concerts, or plays.

The one time my dad did attend an event was when I was fortunate enough to have been selected to take part in a performance of Mahler's Eighth Symphony, often called the "Symphony of a Thousand," at Washington's National Cathedral. We had rehearsed for weeks, and I had learned my lyrics in both English and German. Dad, God bless him, attended and promptly fell asleep.

I returned to Colorado in 1973 and enrolled at the University of Colorado Boulder as a freshman. My gap year had been taken up by working and trying to figure out what I really wanted to do in life.

After that year of working minimum wage jobs, I was more confident in my ability to do well at school and help out in whatever capacity I could in Dad's re-election campaign the following year. I was nineteen years old, and for the first time I was going to be able to do more than stand next to him at a picnic or rally and just look like his cute kid.

We watched over the next summer as the primaries took place on the Democratic side (Dad was unopposed for the Republican primaries), and for the most part felt reasonably comfortable when voters selected Gary Hart as their candidate. We were not the most sophisticated political machine, surely. Dad's advisors and staff were largely close personal friends and acquaintances, and none of us knew what was about to happen.

Hart had been George McGovern's national campaign chairman for the 1972 presidential election and had vetted every state to determine where he'd have the best shot to win a Senate seat. In preparation for his own presidential bid, he picked Colorado. He changed his name along the way from Hartpence to Hart, and moved to Colorado from Nebraska to establish residency.

The 1974 election was a nationwide slaughter of Republicans in the wake of the Watergate scandal and Nixon's resignation. Colorado, and in particular my father, was no exception. My responsibility had been to drum up support for him in Boulder County, since I was then in my second year at the university.

Boulder County is one of the leftest-leaning counties in the history of left-leaning counties, and mine was not a welcome message. The quality and quantity of negativism that spewed my way during those few months left me feeling very bitter and cynical. But Boulder wasn't the only place that happened.

The Hart campaign was extremely well-run and had a

take-no-prisoners attitude. My dad and my family suffered numerous personal attacks which we never had to endure in previous campaigns. It was brutal. The loss devastated my father.

I was invited by a friend to accompany him to Paris after the election, and I grabbed it, wanting to get as far away from Colorado as I could. I left in mid-November, a couple of weeks after the election.

Dad was appointed Ambassador to Switzerland by President Ford, and in early April 1975, he and my mother left the US to take up residence in Bern. He only served five months or so before symptoms of what turned out to be multiple sclerosis became more and more apparent. He resigned and spent the next six years in relative seclusion and decline until his death in 1981.

I spent that time mostly in Paris, attending the American College in Paris and traveling extensively throughout Europe. Together with a small group of American and French friends, I got involved in creating France's first jazz school, the Institute for Artistic and Cultural Perception, and opening an American-style restaurant in the heart of the city called the Top Banana.

I returned to Washington, D.C., in 1979 to finish college. Dad was essentially bed-ridden by then, and I really wanted to honor his one request of me, that I get a college degree. I had one semester left when he died, but at least he knew that I was on my way.

When I finally had children of my own starting in 1989, the issue of fatherhood brought me to question my thoughts about my father, and I concluded that he did the best he could. His main job was work, his career, but he also made very sure the family was well-taken care of.

It bothers me in a kind of abstract way that he was not really present in my life, but I try not to dwell on things over which I have no control. I also do not blame him for my failures. I made the choices in my life that have landed me where I am today, and if anything, his example of strength under adversity and moral rectitude have been very important in my life. Both he and my mother repeatedly stressed the importance of cultivating and hanging onto a sense of humor. Thank God for that! I also appreciate all the opportunities that I had as a result of his life. What a life I have had!

It wasn't until we found the rest of the diary that I was able to see the man he was and understand the why of his career in public service. Maybe the whole created the picture, or maybe I'd finally reached the age where I could be more objective.

I'm incredibly grateful to be who I am, and for the family and friends who have helped me become this person.

Acknowledgements

First and foremost, to my father, who not only survived his ordeal, but also had the presence of mind to write it down. With no diary, there is no book. Thanks, Dad. Your life, and the way you lived it, served as a template for me in my own life. Sometimes you got it absolutely right, and sometimes not so much, but who can say otherwise? My life choices have been mine to make, regardless. Our last moments together have haunted me for years, but as I have managed to forgive you for shutting me out emotionally, so, too, I hope you have forgiven me for asking you in the end to be something you could not be. I love you.

Second, to my beautiful wife, Denise, my soulmate, who gently encouraged me to finish this project, helped with the transcription of part one of the diary, and supported me through the entire process. This would likely not have happened without her love and support.

To my remaining siblings, Michael and Lynne and Peter Jr. (who tragically passed away on New Year's Day 2009) I owe a huge debt. Your stories about Dad, your love and support for me throughout my life, good times and bad, have been instrumental in my becoming who I am today. I love you all.

Finally, to those friends who have offered advice and guidance on the business end of publishing, thanks for your wisdom, your patience, and your support.

www.ingramcontent.com/pod-product-compliance
Lightning Source LLC
Chambersburg PA
CBHW070054120526
44588CB00033B/1429